Given by ...
Principal

D0190049

... on of essays ... cott, brings ... three writers who, in 1915 as throu... lives, were deeply concerned with ... and international peace. Central to the collection is 'Militarism versus Feminism' by C.K. Ogden and Mary Sargant Florence, published as a pamphlet when the First World War was at its height. Catherine Marshall's two shorter essays, 'Women and War' and 'The Future of Women in Politics' shed invaluable light on the links made by the early suffragists between militarism and women's oppression.

CATHERINE E. MARSHALL was born in 1880 and was active in the Women's Liberal Association as early as 1904. She went on to become a principal organiser of the National Union of Women's Suffrage Societies and of its Election Fighting Fund in both working closely with Kathleen D. Courtney. Vigorously opposed to the First World War, she was a prime mover behind the setting up of the international Women's Committee for Permanent Peace which culminated in the Hague Women's Peace Conference of 1915, which the British delegation was prevented from attending when the government closed the North Sea to shipping. Throughout 1916 and 1917, she worked full time for the No-Conscription Fellowship as well as keeping up her interest in the Women's International League, to which she again turned her full attention after the war. Later, she was active on behalf of refugees from fascism.

K. OGDEN was born in 1889, and was a scholar of agdalene College, Cambridge. His espousal of the con...versial issues of his day — feminism and women's ...rage, trade unionism and syndicalism, educational ...rm, atheism and birth control — found its strongest ...ression in his editorship of the *Cambridge Magazine* ...n 1912—21. He was also well known for his work on

Don

aesthetics and the philosophy of language, and especially for the invention of Basic English, a system of linguistic simplification which he hoped would improve communication and understanding between nations.

MARY SARGANT FLORENCE was born in 1857 and is best remembered as a talented painter. She became involved with the suffrage movement prior to the First World War and was a member of the British committee for the Hague Women's Peace Conference. Her contact with C.K. Ogden was made through her son Philip, and she contributed articles to the *Cambridge Magazine* as well as collaborating with Ogden on 'Militarism versus Feminism'.

MARGARET KAMESTER and JO VELLACOTT are researchers at the Simone de Beauvoir Institute, Concordia University, Montreal, where Jo Vellacott also teaches full time in the Women's Studies programme and is currently working on a biography of Catherine Marshall. She is the author of *Bertrand Russell and the Pacifists in the First World War* (Brighton, 1980).

MILITARISM VERSUS FEMINISM:

WRITINGS ON WOMEN AND WAR

CATHERINE MARSHALL,

C.K. OGDEN

AND

MARY SARGANT FLORENCE

EDITED BY

MARGARET KAMESTER

AND

JO VELLACOTT

Published by VIRAGO PRESS Limited 1987
41 William IV Street, London WC2N 4DB

Militarism versus Feminism was first published
in Great Britain 1915 by Allen & Unwin

Introduction copyright © 1987 Margaret Kamester
and Jo Vellacott

British Library Cataloguing in Publication Data
Marshall, Catherine
    Militarism versus feminism : writings
    on women & war.
    1. Women and militarism
    I. Title   II. Florence, Mary Sargant
    III. Ogden, C.K.
    305.4   U21.5

    ISBN 0 – 86068 – 782 – 1

Typeset by Florencetype Limited, Weston-super-Mare
Printed and bound in Great Britain by
Cox & Wyman Ltd., Reading, Berks.

'To Remember the Past is to Commit Oneself to the Future' — Takeshi Araki, Mayor of Hiroshima, at an International Conference on Peace and Security, Montreal, Canada, April 1986

Contents

Acknowledgements

Our small part of this book has benefited from the help of many people, partly in building the background of research out of which it emerged, and partly in direct assistance for the project itself.

Warm thanks to Jill Liddington, as ever, for her encouragement. We also especially appreciate the empowering support of our friends and colleagues at the Simone de Beauvoir Institute, students, Fellows and staff. We are in debt, too, to many feminist and pacifist friends for our growing understanding of issues, and for the climate in which this kind of work is going forward.

We appreciate support for our research received from Concordia University, and we acknowledge with many thanks the friendly and ungrudging help we have received from the following: Inter-library loan and reference services at the Vanier and Norris libraries of Concordia University; reference services at the McLennan library of McGill University; special collections (C.K. Ogden Papers) and the Bertrand Russell archives, McMaster University; Cumbria Record Office (Catherine E. Marshall Papers); the City of

London Polytechnic, Fawcett Collection; Mrs Barbara Halpern; the Western History Collection, University of Colorado (WILPF international archives); the Swarthmore College Peace Collection; the British Library of Political and Economic Science (WIL, Britain, archives).

Introduction

Feminist consciousness: 1900–1914

Early twentieth-century feminism has often been seen so much in terms of the suffrage campaign that we seem to be expected to believe that with the coming of the war in 1914 feminists not only laid aside the struggle for the vote, but stopped thinking altogether. Since a benevolent government gave women the vote at the end of the war, they never had to think again. Writings such as those reprinted here give the lie to this facile view, showing that the war itself and the forcing-house of 1915 clarified radical feminist thought and gave a hard edge to what had been no more than implicit before. The thread of strong, well-articulated pacifist feminism that is revealed here did not, as we all know to our cost, prevail in its time, may in fact have had no numerically large following (though of this we cannot be certain), and had no measurable political impact; but now, at the least, it helps to make sense of the inter-war efforts of pacifist women, most notably the members of the Women's International League for Peace and Freedom. More than that, it is of profound significance to us now, illuminating and validating our own struggles, and even encouraging us to move beyond the point we

1

have reached in our thinking. So many fine things were said so long ago; it is shocking that they disappeared for so many years, but now it is a delight and a privilege to play a small role in the rebirth, relishing the sense which we are regaining of connectedness and hope.

The year 1915 saw a flurry of writing against the war and in favour of social change and of a new international order.[1] The feminist pacifist element in this had important pre-war roots, which we will outline briefly here before going on to say more about the authors and the immediate content of the 1915 writings printed here, one 'of them (we believe) for the first time.

At the beginning of the twentieth century, many women felt themselves to be living in an exciting time, a time of infinite possibility. Throughout most of the western world, middle-class women already benefited from hard-won advances in education, in marriage and property laws, and in work opportunities, while working-class women in at least some areas were gaining experience and confidence in labour struggles and building support networks as workers and consumers, where expression of social and economic needs was possible.

Not surprisingly, women looked towards the vote as the essential next step. It was to be in part a culmination of the century of struggle but in greater part the means of ensuring that women would in future be able to look after their own interests rather than having to rely on men for every necessary change in law. Catherine Marshall,[2] author of two of the essays reprinted here, and long a leading non-militant suffragist, liked to illustrate her suffrage speeches with a fable about an old woman who sent her husband repeatedly to market with instructions, and was as often disappointed and frustrated with his

2

failure to get it exactly right; the moral, of course, was that whatever the anti-suffragists might say, women's interests could not and would not be adequately represented by men.

Adoption of suffrage as an all-important goal led to the downplaying of other issues, but not nearly as completely as myth has represented. The major visible divisions within the British suffrage movement were on strategy (between militancy and non-militancy), and on the structures and process of the suffrage organisations.[3] The emergence among suffrage groups of militants and non-militants, of demagogues and democrats is not surprising, and may in fact have a good deal to tell us about the underlying ideologies and likely political direction of the members of the several suffrage groups. Few wanted to explore these differences at the time. As for party political issues, they were avoided as far as possible within the major national organisations, in the interests of unity, and more firmly still in public stance. Even when members of the Women's Social and Political Union (WSPU) directed verbal and sometimes physical attacks against Liberal government members, they did so solely on grounds of the Party's failure to promote suffrage; even when the National Union of Women's Suffrage Societies (NUWSS) decided to offer direct election support to the Labour Party, in the form of funded campaign organisers, they made it clear that this involved a commitment solely to the suffrage plank in Labour's platform, and was based on the hope of putting pressure on the Liberal government.

None of these attempts to preserve an appearance of unity and political neutrality prevented a great growth of feminist consciousness taking place behind the common front. Of particular interest are the women within the National Union leadership who

3

helped orchestrate the strategic alliance with Labour, and who came to see connections, in those turbulent times of labour troubles and Irish restlessness, between different forms of social oppression.

Another educative feature of pre-war suffragism was its international character. The history of the struggle for the vote within each country has tended to be written up, even by recent feminist writers, as if it existed in isolation,[4] rather than as part of a major movement taking place in remarkably close parallel all over the western world, with a strong international consciousness and support network. The International Women's Suffrage Alliance (IWSA) had been formed in 1904, emerging in part out of an older organisation, the International Council of Women (ICW). The latter had built a widening and effective network on the basis of avoidance of issues that would be controversial within the organisation, and so was not able to adopt women's suffrage. Both organisations fostered friendship across national boundaries, with much inter-visitation and many international gatherings which not only helped break down xenophobia but also did much to build a positive sense of sisterhood and an awareness that the subordination of women went wider and deeper than the mere lack of political enfranchisement.

There was relatively little public debate among British suffragists before 1914 on the issue of a feminist approach to international order and alternatives to war. This may have been in part because it was an issue on which women were not ready to agree, and was also seen as one on which a radical stand would serve only to alienate some needed male political support. Helena Swanwick,[5] editor of the *Common Cause* (the NUWSS journal) from 1909 to 1912, clearly felt that there was an appropriate feminist response to the escalation of war preparations (as

4

in the Dreadnought scare) and believed too that the NUWSS should be prepared to state publicly that militancy was damaging the suffrage cause and was inconsistent in principle with the suffrage goal. Her resignation from the editorship came as a result of her discomfort at the view of some Executive members that these were inappropriate and divisive topics; but she left the position without fanfare, careful to avoid an open split which could harm the Union. She remained on the Executive. In general, however, under her editorship and that of Maude Royden who succeeded her, the *Common Cause* reflected strong and well-considered feminist views on a wide range of issues; its readers were not expected to wait for the vote before becoming socially and politically educated. Far from dropping other feminist concerns, the *Common Cause* publicised and explored everything from wife-battering to unequal pay. Even if the message, implicit or explicit, is always that the vote will help towards solutions, the discussions are not shallow and the issues are treated on their own merits.[6]

Women played a substantial role in the international peace movements that existed in increasing strength throughout the fifty years preceding the First World War. Interestingly, the ICW, for whom suffrage had been too controversial an issue, accepted and supported its own important peace committee, set up on the initiative of the Peace and Arbitration Committee of the American National Council of Women, and chaired by May Wright Sewall.[7] While a number of active suffragists also worked in this and other peace organisations, or followed them with interest, suffrage organisations as such, including the IWSA, steered clear. Mutual interest may well have been served, consciously or unconsciously, on the one hand by suffrage organisations not risking having the women's vote seen as a threat to national military

5

strength, and on the other hand by the peace organisations not becoming identified as representing a
womanish viewpoint or being just another part of the
alarming campaign for women's equality.[8]

Nevertheless, there were women making their
voices heard in the pre-war peace movements as
individuals, in women-only groups, and in mixed
organisations; and from time to time some had linked
the peace or disarmament message powerfully with
the need to improve women's position. Sandi Cooper
adduces evidence that women were heard and well
received, as individuals, in the pre-war European
peace movement.[9]

This may be the other side of a phenomenon which
(perhaps understandably) has been little commented
on by feminist historians, but which is essential
as background to the documents reprinted in this
book; there were in Britain, for instance, at least
undercurrents of male opinion which have every
right to be called feminist. The term was not earned,
and might well have been rejected, by many of those
male parliamentarians who supported women's suffrage from time to time and for various reasons
(often self-serving); but there is no other word for
such men as H.N. Brailsford,[10] Philip Snowden,[11]
Keir Hardie,[12] and George Lansbury,[13] all of whom
served the suffrage cause in ways which showed no
mere vague ideological acceptance of the principle of
equality, much less a calculated self-interest, but a real
respect for the women they worked with and an
understanding of the relevance of their cause.

Alongside this political element, there was also a
climate among some intellectuals, by no means universal but significant nonetheless, in which a kind of
recognition of women was taken as a given — though
at times an ill thought-out given, more honoured in
the breach than in the observance. The Bloomsbury

6

group and the Cambridge intellectuals both come in this category. Bertrand Russell,[14] who always liked to be active on behalf of his beliefs, gave time to work for the NUWSS between 1908 and 1910, before deciding to go for adult suffrage (which, at that time, in our view, was a route to nowhere),[15] and there is plenty in the much-preserved correspondence of the time that shows women's position to have been an actively discussed issue; but Bloomsburians at large were not given to activism. This inconclusive intellectualising and good will may seem frustrating (perhaps Virginia Woolf found it to be so), but it is better than often prevails, and it meant that there was a forum for any who were prepared to take the issues seriously. C.K. Ogden, as we shall see, was not only both liberated and a liberator, but indeed a courageous activist of the pen. One of our interesting discoveries in the course of preparing this book, incidentally, has been the breadth of material he found to draw on; there was more proto-feminist writing around at the turn of the century than we had realised.

Catherine E. Marshall and the move towards radicalism

The story of one of our authors, Catherine E. Marshall, can be told here both for her direct role in pre-war feminist developments, and also as an embodiment of much that we have said about the threads in feminism and internationalism that were to come together in 1914 as stark opposition to militarism.

Catherine Marshall, born in 1880 into a well-to-do and intellectual liberal family,[16] was educated privately in Harrow (her father was a housemaster at Harrow boys' school) and at St Leonard's School, St Andrew's. A number of her women friends went on to Oxford or Cambridge, but for reasons which seem to have had more to do with uncertainty about her health than with prejudice,[17] Catherine did not go to university, although she went on studying history, languages, and music, and she travelled. There were, however, long periods spent at home with her mother and father, who had now retired to a house beside Derwentwater, in the English Lake District. Her parents certainly gave her more freedom than may have been common for young women of her class at that time; she went, for example, on cycling tours in Europe with her younger brother, and for ten days in the Lake District with a woman friend. Yet she had no real independence, never seems to have expected to hold a paid job or pursue a profession, and was subject to a great deal of control and interference, often based on concern for her health, which however genuinely caring (and it was) must strike us as more and more inappropriate as Catherine moved into and through her thirties.

The Suffrage movement was Catherine Marshall's salvation. She and her mother, Caroline, had been active with the Women's Liberal Association (WLA) in Harrow as early as 1904, and had made suffrage a priority even then. In 1908 they worked together, with active support from Catherine's father, Frank, to found the Keswick Women's Suffrage Association (KWSA), affiliated to the NUWSS. From this Catherine moved on to regional organisation and then to work with the national headquarters. She quickly became valued and respected for her energy, intelligence and outstanding ability as an organiser. She demonstrated a keen sense of structure and process and, together with Kathleen Courtney,[18] helped plan and implement changes that made the NUWSS much more democratic, representative and responsive to women's suffrage opinion across class lines. The resilience of the NUWSS in face of the repeated disappointments of 1910−13, and the sophistication of its organisation and strategy, owed a great deal to these two,[19] and it was they who played a major part, working with H.N. Brailsford, in the election alliance with the Labour Party (known as the Election Fighting Fund), which was the new strategy of 1913−14.[20]

For Catherine Marshall, this new move and the close contact it brought with working-class suffragists and with trade unionists (male and female) was enormously educational, coming as it did just as she was questioning the idealistic L/liberalism with which she had grown up. Much as this questioning may have begun with disillusionment at the reluctance of the Liberal government to take up the suffrage issue, it was also fed by a sense that the issues had outgrown the old parties and even the old theories. In a private interview with Sir Edward Grey[21] in December 1913, she spoke of the coming struggle between capital and labour, outlined the interconnectedness of women's position and that of the workers, and referred to 'kinship with subject races', saying, 'it matters enormously to the whole future civilisation whether these 3 movements run on sound lines, or are driven into revolution. *The women will have great effect on both.*' The women's influence, she added, 'ought to be a steadying effect'; and she spoke of the international consequences: 'It will affect [the] W[omen's] M[ovement] *all over the world what example we set in England . . . how* we win the vote here.'[22] This is radical stuff, and makes radical connections; it is not the voice of a woman who merely wants admission to the male-dominated system or even equality within it; it is the voice of a woman who believes that a new system must be developed, and a new spirit within that system.

When Britain declared war on Germany on 4 August 1914, Catherine Marshall was in London, very busy with the meeting of the Executive of the IWSA. The impact of the outbreak of the war cannot be recaptured in a few words. Circumstances (a divided Cabinet, an intransigent and too well-prepared military among them) had combined to keep the imminence of war under wraps.

Perhaps the least confused were the various shades of militarists, from generals to public school boys who saw an opportunity for glory or adventure. If they had been able to look beyond 1914, what would they have seen? Many of the young men, we know, would have seen a world in which they person-ally would play no part, a world from which death would shortly remove them; but, as ever, this is some-thing to which imagination does not easily lend itself. And looking beyond 1918, to 1939, to 1945, to the 1980s, would the generals and the statesmen have rejoiced at the continuation of power politics, at the escalation of militarism, at the expenditures on weapons of war, at the entrenchment of 'big stick' diplomacy? Logically, they should rejoice: but per-haps such a clear vision of the future came, when it came, only to the radical dissidents; we are constantly struck by the accuracy of their unheeded prophecies.

As for the liberal internationalists, until the last minute they hoped and believed that 'their' party, in power, would maintain British neutrality and put the country in a position to act as a peacemaker in the European conflict. When war came, some leapt to the defence of the party, others felt betrayed.[23] Working-class suffragists such as Selina Cooper,[24] international socialists, and those sometime liberal feminists who were already well on their way towards some form of socialist feminism, such as Marshall, saw their hopes of solidarity across international boundaries dashed. For the suffragists, the bitterness of the shock must have been increased by the immediate irony of the

10

IWSA gathering, by the bridges they were even then building among women, and which they now saw blown up.[25]

Another feature of August 1914, hard to recapture across the years, is the almost universal belief that, terrible as the war might be (and not all thought this), it would be brief ('six weeks', they said, 'we'll have the boys home by Christmas', they said). In this climate, the NUWSS offered co-operation in combating the disorganisation caused by the war. Since the government had its plans ready for the British Expeditionary Force but had little indeed set up to deal with critical economic dislocation at home, the large pool of effective women organisers of the NUWSS was a welcome resource.[26] Individually and corporately some of the leading members took on tasks related to the alleviation of suffering, at the same time refusing involvement in recruiting (taken up with enthusiasm by Emmeline and Christabel Pankhurst), and continuing the National Union's role of monitor and advocate in women's causes. For instance, the *Common Cause* and/or the NUWSS Executive attacked attempts to reintroduce the notorious Contagious Diseases Acts by military regulation, to exclude women factory workers from pubs (often the only handy shelter available in shift breaks), to use the pool of female labour to downgrade wages, to employ women without giving them the training men would have had, to supervise serving men's wives to ascertain their moral fitness to receive the separation allowance, and to discourage eager middle-class volunteers from taking jobs from women who needed to be paid to do them. Marshall took an interest in all of these issues.

At the beginning of September, Marshall accepted a position — a government job[27] — as Secretary of the Sub-Committee of the Queen's Committee for Employment of Women, but stuck to her decision to help out in this way for one month only.[28] She took a much-needed short holiday in October, and this may well have helped her to turn her thoughts to the broader issues involved in the war. Not that these had ever been totally submerged, despite the busyness of the early weeks; she and a number of women suffragists in many countries on both sides of the Atlantic had found in the outbreak of war an appalling logic: this was what happened in a world where women were excluded from decision-making and female skills and characteristics were undervalued.

Yet most publicly articulate Britons appear to have accepted the war as out of their hands and as demanding patriotic sacrifice on their parts. There may well have been more latent dissent than we can ever hope to pinpoint;[29] but on the surface Britons were behind the war effort. Young men enlisted in droves, women nobly sacrificed their husbands and sons and mourned the dead with pride.

Those women and men who could not accept this traditional view of warfare had begun to seek each other out even in the first confusing days of the war, but for the first few months opposition to the war had been muted. The Union of Democratic Control,[30] one of the first groups to form in response to the war, and the internationalist or pacifist feminists were alike working for improved understanding and a better international structure to be implemented after the war's end. By late 1914, however, talk of a brief war was over; shortages, long casualty lists, naval and civilian losses at sea, shelling of civilians and trench warfare were fulfilling the worst fears of those who had known that this war would be quantitatively and qualitatively far more devastating than previous wars. With the escalation of the real atrocities always attendant upon war, and the even greater escalation of atrocity stories (whichever side one was on, all evil

12

deeds were of course committed by the other side),[31] thoughtful people became more outspoken on the urgent need for better structures and better understanding.

In *Jus Suffragii*, 1 November 1914, Mary Sheepshanks[32] wrote in a remarkable editorial, 'Patriotism or Internationalism':

In all this orgy of blood ... what are the women doing? They are, as is the lot of women, binding up the wounds that men have made. ... But that is not enough. ... Women must not only use their hands to bind up, they must use their brains to understand the causes of the European frenzy, and their lives must be devoted to putting a stop for ever to such wickedness ... we must earnestly study the causes of the present criminal madness. False patriotic pride and love of conquest ... must go. ... Armaments must be drastically reduced and abolished, and their place taken by an international peace force. Instead of two great Alliances pitted against each other, we must have a true Concert of Europe. Peace must be on generous, unvindictive lines, satisfying legitimate national needs, and leaving no cause for resentment such as to lead to another war. Only so can it be permanent.

And in the *Common Cause* for 20 November, an unsigned leading article entitled 'A Sacred Trust' asks:

Is it not, then, a sacred trust for us to build up public opinion in such wise that if and when our rulers are in a position to consider terms of peace, they will find behind them a great and mighty force making for justice, for self-control, for wisdom?

While many feminists, female and male, saw women as having distinct and complementary qualities to contribute, they seldom labelled men as inherently

13

militaristic nor women as inevitably nurturing; Marshall, for instance, condemned a value system, to be found in no matter which sex, which turned on power to dominate and impose one's will on others. The feminist language of the time, with its heavy emphasis on an almost mystical quality of mothering, should not blind us to the radical nature of what was being said. Catherine Marshall and like-minded women based their claim to equal political rights on the different experience of women, claiming that with half the human race excluded, half of human qualities were under-represented and undervalued.

Increasingly, Marshall was giving her attention to the conditions which might form the basis of a lasting peace, and lost no opportunity of talking about these in detail with her pre-war Cabinet contacts.[33] At the same time, talks she was asked to give on 'Women in Wartime' became focused on the obligation of women to stand against the jingoistic outcry of the time. We find Marshall and others, notably Helena Swanwick and Isabella Ford,[34] like Mary Sheepshanks, stressing their fear that no good peace could be made in a climate of atrocity stories and escalating hatred. Unfortunately, the issue was controversial. It had been clear, from the beginning of the war, that the NUWSS Executive was divided in its response to the war.[35] Millicent Fawcett[36] and her closest suppor-ters[37] feared what they saw as an unpatriotic trend, which they identified with the policy of the Union of Democratic Control, an organisation whose sensible platform and patient approach seems in retrospect to have been excessively moderate, if not positively timid, but which was publicly and violently attacked as traitorous.

Two issues focused the disagreement within the NU. The first was growing pressure from the 'pacifist' group to have the NU consider it as part of its feminist work to plan for a satisfactory peace. Few were able in the first few months of the war to make the connection between feminism and anti-militarism quite as conclusively as it is made in the articles reprinted in this book, but they were increasingly clear that there *was* a connection. Voteless women had had no power to prevent this terrible war, but that was not all; militarism by its nature implied the subservience of women, and a strong free woman-hood was antithetical to militarism. Although it was not always couched in these terms, the argument was really about whether women would prove themselves responsible citizens by accepting the male-defined support roles in peace and war, agreeing to bear and nurture the warriors; or whether they would insist on taking their supposed predisposition to nurturing and conciliation into the decision-making sphere, and have the preservation of life become an important consideration in international relations.

Within the NUWSS Executive the cracks could not be papered over for long, and an agreement which they had entered into, to refrain from 'official' public comment on the war-related questions on which they were divided, was proving unrealistic. Millicent Fawcett, in particular, was seen by the 'pacifist' element as breaching the understanding on more than one occasion. Meanwhile, the debate about feminist education for peace heated up from October 1914 to February 1915, when it was brought to a national council meeting. While considerable support was articulated, Marshall and K.D. Courtney felt that nothing concrete had been accepted, and both re-signed from the Executive.

The proposal for a women's international peace conference posed a further challenge to the NUWSS leadership. The International Women's Suffrage Association had been planning to hold its regular (usually biennial) conference in the spring of 1915, and when the IWSA decided to cancel this the proposal was soon made, by Dr Aletta Jacobs of Holland,[38] that an international gathering of women should still be held, at which alternatives to war would be the topic. Catherine Marshall was one of those who met with a small planning committee at the Hague in February 1915 to bring the conference about.[39] In the event, it was enthusiastically supported by many suffragists on both sides of the Atlantic, but by few organisations as such.

In the NUWSS, Millicent Fawcett set herself firmly against it, and gained enough support that those leading members of the NUWSS who thought the Hague conference an important development, deserving of their commitment, felt they had no choice but to resign. More than half of the Executive gave up their positions, while retaining their membership in the NUWSS. A number of them moved immediately into work for the International Women's Committee for Permanent Peace, as the conference organisation was called.

The Hague International Women's Conference of April 1915 was an astonishing achievement, bringing together in a time of war women from both sides of the Atlantic and, more remarkably, from both sides of the conflict, as well as from neutral nations. There was no lack of doomsayers. Many, including Fawcett, held that it would be impossible for women of opposing nations to meet together without breaking up in bitter recriminations. More held that it *ought* to be impossible, that the wish to try was in itself unpatriotic. The planners of the conference, aware of the danger, set as a ground rule that no discussion would be allowed on the subject of national responsibility for the outbreak of war, or on the conduct of the war. In the event, while there were some lively and even

16

heated exchanges, these ground rules and the good faith of the participants cleared the way for much constructive work, accomplished in a spirit of good will. The story is available, though for many years it has not been nearly as well known as it deserves to be.[40]

As many as 180 British women wanted to attend the conference. The government first stated that no one could go, then chose twenty-eight to whom they would issue passports, but announced at almost the same time that the North Sea was closed to all shipping. Only three women, all of whom had already left England, were able to be present; one of them was Kathleen Courtney, who had also been on the planning committee. Jane Addams,[41] already very well known in the United States for her reform and peace work, chaired the conference, and was one of several women who took the resulting resolutions to heads of state and foreign ministers in almost all the capitals of Europe, as well as to the President of the United States. With the resolutions went a plan, drawn up by Julia Grace Wales, a Canadian at the University of Wisconsin, for continuous mediation by neutrals as a step towards bringing the belligerents to the conference table.[42] Statesmen showed an interest which we believe was more than mere politeness; but no one was found to take the initiative.

In England, the Hague conference attracted considerable attention in the press, not least among those who despised its objectives and mocked the 'peacettes', a name given by the *Daily Express* to the unfortunate women who were stranded at Tilbury when the North Sea was closed.[43] But for the anti-war movement it provided a splendid renewal. The discussions, even the controversy, which had preceded it had stimulated supportive interest as well as criticism. The debacle of the British women's failure to get to

17

Holland evoked sympathy for the delegates and anger at the government, as well as contempt. The reports brought back from the conference, and by the travelling delegates on their visits to heads of state, were greeted with enthusiasm by other peace people, some of whom were feeling great frustration with endless polite peace gatherings at which intellectuals held forth on long-term solutions with little reference to the realities of the appalling carnage.[44]

Women's peace efforts spurred others to consider the relation between women and militarism. Catherine Marshall was invited to speak in March 1915 at a gathering to examine aims in the religious context; the talk on 'Women and War' printed in this book was prepared for this occasion. It is cast in a more religious tone than was usual for her, but the message contains much that she had been urging since November 1914.[45] The other piece by Marshall included here, 'The Future of Women in Politics', is an exposition of ideas very dear to her. Her pre-war experience had led her to see an alliance between women and labour as immensely important, going far beyond the pre-war limited strategic pact made by the NUWSS with the Labour Party. Her sense that the war was not made by women or workers, and was not in the interests of either, made more urgent her desire to see close co-operation between these two groups, to work for a changed world. She recognised, however, some of the deep problems involved, and in this paper, specifically addressed to members of the Labour Party, she spelled out clearly the difficulties inherent in the long-term sex-role socialisation of men to dominance and competition. She warned, too, of the danger of embarking on class warfare in place of international antagonism. The future she saw for women in politics was as initiators of a radical new spirit, the spirit of co-operation.

Curiously, we know of no direct connection or even meeting between C.K. Ogden and Marshall; but their writings and Marshall's speaking, and the influence of the Hague conference, are like torches in a spreading illumination, one catching fire from another and all lighting up the relationship between the long suffrage campaign and the life-and-death struggle between militarism and feminism.

One solid outcome of the Hague conference was the formation, immediately afterwards, of the Women's International League (WIL), later the British section of WILPF (which did not take the name until 1919). Marshall was an active member of WIL, and throughout 1915 she spent most of her time working for it, alongside Helena Swanwick, the first president. At the end of that year, when conscription was imminent, she worked for the National Council Against Conscription and then for the No Conscription Fellowship,[46] to which she eventually gave the bulk of her time in 1916 and 1917. For much of 1918, she was incapacitated by a severe illness, resulting in part from overwork.

Marshall and the spirit of 1915 were to meet up again in 1919, when the post-war conference which the Hague participants had promised themselves took place in Zurich. Once the League of Nations was set up and established in Geneva, WILPF made its headquarters there, at the Maison Internationale, where Marshall worked for much of 1920 and 1921, becoming very well informed on economic reconstruction, on the Irish situation, and on proposals for treaty revision, as well as on the functioning and limitations of the League itself. When in England, she concerned herself with the policies and prospects of the Labour Party, being approached on one occasion to run as a candidate, which she declined. The brilliance of her earlier political work no longer came easily to her and frequent illness intervened; nevertheless she continued to occupy herself with causes she deemed important. In the late 1930s she began a strenuous period of work for Jewish refugees from Czechoslovakia, and the evil she saw in Nazism led her to modify her absolute pacifist stance and to withdraw temporarily from active membership in WILPF. Until her death, she followed the work of the Labour Party, the UDC, and later the United Nations Organisation, keeping up a lively correspondence.

As for WILPF, what had been begun at the Hague has continued to this day, although largely unsung. A great deal of solid and fascinating work was done between the wars by national and international sections but, as in Marshall's own case, confrontation with the absolute evil of Nazism — whose genesis they had hoped to prevent by treaty revision and economic reconstruction — posed problems which were hard to resolve. In the case of WILPF, the resultant internal divisions and indecisiveness were debilitating; there was still an important message to give but the flame to light its way was burning low.

Now that we have the benefit of a longer view and can perhaps see better the place of the pacifist thought of 1915 in the development of feminist theory and action, we can hope to take it and use it again. Perhaps we may yet be able to say of the whole 1915 phenomenon, as C.K. Ogden said of the Hague congress, that it 'will stand out as one of the landmarks of modern history. With this event . . . begins a new era in the annals of feminism.'[47]

The Background to *Militarism versus Feminism*

Authorship and publication

Readers of the *Cambridge Magazine*, published in Britain during the years 1912—21, expressed a good deal of curiosity about the mysterious writer, Adelyne More, whose name appeared at the head of many articles included in its pages. One of these articles was the last section of one of a series of studies on the influence of war on the position of women,[48] which became part of the anonymous work, *Militarism versus Feminism*, published by Allen & Unwin in April 1915. We would love to be able to produce the evidence that Adelyne More was yet another forgotten feminist and the sole author of the book. However, this was merely one of the several pseudonyms used by C.K. Ogden, the editor of the *Cambridge Magazine*. The name began as a pun, but was taken so seriously by readers that Ogden, with typical tongue-in-cheek humour, was later moved to insert in the magazine the notice of Miss More's white wedding at Great St Mary's Church;[49] his friend I.A. Richards later recalled, 'I believe I dissuaded him from announcing triplets'.[50]

But it is clear from the prefatory note to the *Cambridge Magazine* series that Ogden was not the only author involved. Further material from the book appeared between January and March 1915 in two other periodicals, the *Common Cause*,[51] where C.K. Ogden is given as the author, and *Jus Suffragii*,[52] where another name appears with Ogden's — Mary Sargant Florence: no pseudonym this time, but a well-known artist and suffragist whose son, Philip, was C.K. Ogden's colleague and friend at Cambridge.

Correspondence between Ogden and the publishers in March and April 1915[53] shows that Ogden was the leading protagonist in the writing of the work; indeed, he himself undertook its production, as much of it was 'in type already standing' for his *Cambridge Magazine*, with Allen & Unwin claiming a commission on the sales but no other fee. A favourable reaction to the articles by readers of the three periodicals and the feeling of urgency among antimilitarists after the first winter of the war apparently encouraged him to seek a wider public for their message as speedily as possible; as stated in the prefatory note to *Militarism versus Feminism*, it was hoped to publish a fuller version later on. The first mention of the project by Allen & Unwin is made in a letter to Ogden on 10 March; agreement on terms was reached on 15 March; the proofs went to the printer on 30 March, and *Militarism versus Feminism* was published on 19 April. Accounts sent to Ogden by Allen & Unwin show that by the end of 1916 just over 1,000 copies had been sold — at sixpence a copy certainly no one made their fortune from it; it was not reprinted, and by March 1918 the publishers note in a letter that the work has been out of print for some time.

C.K. Ogden

Who, then, was this male writer who so eloquently espoused the cause of the feminist pacifists in the early months of the 1914—18 war? Charles Kay Ogden (1889—1957) is described in his obituary in *The Times* as 'an unconventional but deeply learned and profoundly original thinker'.[54] He was a scholar of Magdalene College, Cambridge, but his academic career seems to have played second fiddle to other activities: first, as a founder and leading light of the Heretics, a society for which the touchstone of membership was the rejection of authority on religious truths. Here papers were read on a wide range of topics in religion, politics, philosophy and literature by such prominent intellectuals as George

22

Bernard Shaw, G.K. Chesterton, and Rupert Brooke. C.K., as he was known to all his friends, 'took it for granted that women undergraduates should be equal members of the Society and of its government'.[55]

Secondly, in 1912 he became editor of the *Cambridge Magazine*. The editorial offices were originally in Ogden's room, a 'fantastically cluttered' attic over a fish shop, known as 'Top Hole'.[56] From its beginnings, the magazine reflected the wide interests of its editors; his friend Philip Sargant Florence said that Ogden was 'not a party man ... but picked out certain issues as important. Most of them were unpopular; feminism and women's suffrage, trade unionism and syndicalism ... international peace ... educational reform ... atheism and birth control'.[57] By 1915, Ogden was obviously well known to and in close touch with the anti-militarists among the leaders of the suffrage movement.[58] In later years, his magazine continued to discuss controversial issues like birth control and to publicise the unequal status of women in the university which persisted long after the vote was won.

From 1916 to 1918, the *Cambridge Magazine* each month published an exhaustive and balanced review of the foreign press, unique in wartime Britain, for which it became widely known − and also unpopular with the establishment, although it was never anti-British. 'Notes from the Foreign Press' was edited by Mrs C.R. Buxton, aided by 'a group of keen translators, many of them University graduates or undergraduates'.[59] With its freely expressed anti-militarist sympathies, this resulted in several verbal confrontations (or 'rumpuses', as C.K. like to call them) in the pages of the magazine during the war years,[60] and on 11 November 1918 the *Cambridge Magazine* Book Shop and Art Gallery were wrecked by students 'celebrating' the Armistice.[61] An evaluation of Ogden's

23

multi-faceted career, written after his death, suggests that the comparative lack of recognition which was his lot was at least partly because 'the majority of the Cambridge Establishment did not like his attitude to the war'.[62]

The *Cambridge Magazine*, however, retained its 'cheerful strength of mind and sense of purpose';[63] it was re-established in London, became a quarterly, and later merged with the periodical *Psyche*, under which guise it continued to be a forum for Ogden's many interests. These interests were principally reflected in the 1920s by the publication of prestigious books on the *Foundations of Aesthetics*[64] (with I.A. Richards and James Wood) and *The Meaning of Meaning*[65] (with I.A. Richards — referred to by the authors as *Beadig of Beadig* 'in memory of a frustrating cold in the head').[66] The germ of this latter book on the philosophy of language is found in Ogden's close friendship with Victoria Lady Welby from 1910 until her death in 1912 at the age of seventy-five.[67] Lady Welby was god-daughter and Maid of Honour to Queen Victoria; in her youth she travelled extensively with her mother and later became a formidable and respected scholar, specialising in the science of meaning and the theory of (linguistic) signs, which she called 'significs'. Her book, *Grains of Sense*, published in 1897, contained the following words:

The mutual deafness, dumbness and blindness which is the mental condition of our 'Modern Babel' ... must indeed make terribly for war ... Few things indeed would be likely to do more to further the prospects of universal peace, than a general expansion ... of linguistic converse between all civilized nations.[68]

Ogden's interest in significs, aroused by this friendship and a voluminous correspondence, not only resulted in *The Meaning of Meaning*, but led on to the work for which he is most famous, the development of *Basic English*. This was a programme of linguistic simplification which he believed would increase the ease and accuracy of communication and therefore of understanding between nations; during the 1930s over thirty branches of the programme were established internationally, and in the 1940s it received government support in Britain: Winston Churchill sponsored it and gave a speech at Harvard in September 1943 describing Basic English as a 'very carefully wrought plan for an international language capable of very wide transactions'.[69]

Ogden was also known as the editor of several series of books, notably Kegan Paul's *International Library of Psychology, Philosophy and Scientific Method*, and the *History of Civilisation*. His work as a translator ranged from Romain Rolland's *Au Dessus de la Melée* (*Above the Battle*), which is quoted so effectively in the final pages of *Militarism versus Feminism*,[70] to Wittgenstein's *Tractacus Logico−Philosophicus* on which he collaborated with F.P. Ramsey, and which 'brought a new dimension of philosophy to Cambridge scholarship'.[71]

Possessor of a brilliant, original, witty but nonetheless deep intellect, Ogden was also a 'sensitive and kindly man',[72] beloved and respected by many friends of both sexes, an ally whom feminists and pacifists did not hesitate to acknowledge. But it is probably not by chance that neither his biographies in the *Dictionary of National Biography* and *Who Was Who 1951−1960* nor his obituary in *The Times* mentions his involvement with these movements during the First World War. Regarded as of no importance by a patriarchal and militaristic establishment, his work in this sphere deserves recognition and remembrance.

Mary Sargant Florence (1857–1954) was a prominent artist: not prominent enough (or perhaps of the wrong sex) for an entry in the *Dictionary of National Biography*, but reading her obituaries in *Who Was Who 1951–1960* and *The Times*,[73] we see that she shares with Ogden the dubious distinction of having her feminist and pacifist activities completely ignored. Turning to the *Suffrage Annual and Women's Who's Who for 1913*,[74] and to the letters of her daughter-in-law, the American feminist Lella Secor,[75] we can begin to fill in some of the gaps.

Mary Sargant was one of a large and distinguished family, the daughter of an eminent barrister. A sister, Ethel (1863–1918), was a respected botanist, closely connected with Girton College, Cambridge. Of four brothers, Charles followed his father's profession successfully enough to be knighted and made a member of the Privy Council. Francis was a well-known sculptor (typically, Mary Sargant's entry in a dictionary of artists begins by referring to her as 'the sister of sculptor F.W. Sargant').[76] In 1888 she married an American musician, Henry Smyth Florence, and her son and daughter, Philip and Alix, were born in New Jersey; when her husband died in 1892, she returned to England with her two small children. She lived for most of the rest of her life in a house of her own design and decoration – 'Lord's Wood', in Marlow, Buckinghamshire; her recreations are described as 'gardening and suffrage meetings'.[77]

It is not clear when Mary Sargant Florence's involvement with the women's suffrage movement began, but by 1913 she was a member of the National Union, the Women's Freedom League and the Women's Tax Resistance League, and had been 'twice sold up to protest against taxation without representation'.[78]

In 1915 she was a member of the British general committee for the Women's International Congress at the Hague,[79] and was in correspondence with Helena Swanwick, expressing her wish to 'co-operate with feminist-pacifists'.[80] She evidently sympathised strongly with the conscientious objectors, and in 1916 wrote to Bertrand Russell voicing her concern and offering her home as a retreat from the intensive work he was then doing for the No Conscription Fellowship.[81]

Her initial contact with C.K. Ogden was most likely made through her son Philip. Mary Sargant Florence corresponded with Ogden and contributed articles to the *Cambridge Magazine* on the subject of colour theory;[82] she worked out a 'harmony compass', a complex series of relations between colours and musical harmonies, in which he was much interested. Her speciality as an artist, however, was in large mural decoration and in 'the difficult medium of "true fresco" . . . Very few modern artists have mastered this technique, in which Mrs Sargant-Florence may be said to have challenged the saying of Michelangelo that oil painting is for women and fresco for men'.[83] Her best-known works are a panel in tempera at Chelsea Town Hall, and decorations in fresco at the Old School, Oakham, Rutland,[84] where another brother, Walter, was headmaster for many years. She was editor of the *Papers, vol. 3, 1925–1935*, of the Society of Painters in Tempera, and in 1940 finally published her work on colour co-ordination in a book of that title.[85] As early as 1914, a discussion of women painters included the judgement that 'Among the painters of large decorative designs who exhibit in England, Mary Sargant Florence surely stands in the first rank with her strange, bold, original figures, and admirable effects of calculated perspective.'[86]

As a personality, Sargant Florence remains shadowy; the most intimate glimpses we have of her

27

come from her daughter-in-law's letters, though even these are rather circumspect, being addressed to Lella's family in America. However, we do find a charming description of 'Mother Florence' as 'quite tiny, with dreamy blue eyes and sort of autumn coloured hair which is constantly escaping from her little top knot and hanging in ringlets about her face and neck. She is rather scornful of clothes . . .'[87] The editor of the letters, however, informs us that

although Mary Sargant Florence was delighted to have a daughter-in-law with such advanced views politically, the two women never saw eye to eye on clothes, child care or general comfort . . . Lella thought her mother-in-law both Spartan and impractical, found her insistence on fresh air and early rising a trial, and her sense of humour entirely lacking.[88]

(The invasion of 'Lord's Wood' in 1919 by Lella and Philip and two small sons after Mary had had many years of comparative solitude, although it was not a permanent arrangement, may account for the lack of a sense of humour.)

These, then, were the two known authors of *Militarism versus Feminism*. We have no way of knowing which parts of the text were by one or the other — still less of discovering who others of the 'several collaborators' might be.[89] Perhaps this was just Ogden's way of acknowledging his debt to other writers such as Helena Swanwick, whose work he has obviously studied carefully.[90] A letter to Ogden from Maude Royden,[91] editor of the *Common Cause*, refers to 'Mrs Florence's piece', sent to her for possible publication, but evidently returned as the policy of the paper was just then changing owing to the split in the National Union. This piece may well be part of the book, but which part we cannot guess.

Not surprisingly, the mainstream press of the day did not react favourably (when it reacted at all) to the publication of *Militarism versus Feminism*. A review in the *Times Literary Supplement*[92] grants that the 'enquiry' (of the subtitle) 'is conducted with ability and a good deal of knowledge' but criticises the 'policy' as vague, and goes on to state categorically that 'the spirit of violence' will always 'have to be resisted by force', and that feminists above all others should realise this, as 'their most prominent representatives ... have ... made violence a deliberate and continuous feature in public and social life'. (One understands why the constitutional suffragists of the National Union were so afraid of the damage done to their cause by the militant suffragettes and had come to dissociate themselves from their activities.) The review concludes with the remark that women in wartime cannot be said to be a 'negligible factor', because 'it is war which gives women a unique opportunity for finding the one activity — outside the home and the training of the young — which man is not as well suited to succeed in as she is — viz., nursing.' So much for the establishment press of early 1915!

In other circles, *Militarism versus Feminism* received more favourable attention, and was naturally well publicised in the periodicals in which it had been serialised. The *Ethical World*, a magazine published in London from 1907–16, printed a review in June 1915 by C. Delisle Burns,[93] which praises the original ideas of the authors on such important issues and wonders only that the women's movement had not earlier made the vital connection between militarism in society and their own lack of progress.

About Militarism, Feminism and the Birthrate

Reference has already been made to the extended version of the book which Ogden had hoped to publish. It remains among his papers, almost complete, incorporating most of the text of *Militarism versus Feminism* and showing the results of extensive further research on the position of women in primitive society, among the Iroquois, in Greece and Rome, China, Japan, India, and in Europe from the Middle Ages to the twentieth century. Again and again the main thesis — that the more militaristic the society, the lower the status of women — is shown to be true. Points already made in *Militarism versus Feminism* are further developed, and the train of thought evolves into some striking passages, from which we have included some short excerpts at the end of the main text. The penultimate chapter was to consist of a survey of the different manifestations of the women's peace movement — a full report of the Hague congress and of the Women's Peace Party in the United States, and material on the Women's Group of the Ethical Movement and the Women's Union for Peace (of which a leader was Norah O'Shea, one of the anti-militarists in the National Union) — as well as a historical discussion of women's attempts to stop armed conflicts, ranging from an incident in the Civil War in seventeenth-century England to the work of Frederica Bremer[94] and Bertha von Suttner,[95] and ending with extended quotations from Helena Swanwick's pamphlet, *Women and War*, which she wrote in 1915 for the Union of Democratic Control. The opening and concluding chapters are almost identical to the introduction and chapter five of *Militarism versus Feminism*.

The question remains: why did Ogden not proceed with the publication of this manuscript? The answer can perhaps be found in the emergence of a new theme in his work — a protest against the view of women as breeding machines which made its inevitable appearance under wartime conditions. Several references are made to this theme in *Militarism versus Feminism*;[96] it is reflected in the title given to the longer manuscript — *Militarism, Feminism and the Birthrate* — and is expanded quite extensively in a chapter called 'Food for Cannon'. It is most fully treated in the next publication in which he had a hand — *Fecundity and Civilisation: Overpopulation as the Cause of War and the Chief Obstacle to the Emancipation of Women*. So it seems probable that as this new emphasis came to have over-riding importance for the authors, a new work altogether was begun, resulting in the publication of *Fecundity and Civilisation* and the other manuscript remaining unfinished.

This subject was indeed of urgent concern to feminists in 1915—16. There was a definite policy of governments in Europe, and to some extent in Britain, to encourage soldiers leaving for the front to marry and beget children, and this was strongly protested by anti-militarists everywhere. For example, in the *Common Cause* for 4 December 1914, an article on 'War and the Birthrate' quotes an American doctor:

The crowning infamy of this war . . . is the attitude of European governments in urging men to wed as a matter of patriotic duty . . . This is done in the interests of a high birthrate by governments which are wholly indifferent to the highest death rate . . . This is to ask [woman] to immolate her body and to sink the highest and holiest instinct of womanhood at the bidding of ruthless war.

Again in the *Common Cause* for 30 April 1915, Maude Royden writes on 'Morals and Militarism', deploring the printed slips being circulated in Britain urging men 'to forego no opportunity of paternity', and calling this policy 'the reduction of woman to the status of mere breeders of the race'. One very striking protest is referred to in *Militarism, Feminism and the Birthrate*: a one-act play or melodrama entitled 'War Brides'.[97] Set in a nameless European village, the main character, pregnant by a husband to whom she had been betrothed long before the war, scorns the credulity of the village girls who regard as romantic and patriotic their hasty mass marriages with iron wedding rings to soldiers leaving for the front; when she hears of her husband's death, she shoots herself rather than bear a child as cannon fodder.

Also quoted is a striking speech by Emmeline Pethick-Lawrence,[98] which today's readers must find almost unbearably prophetic. She is discussing an article in the *Daily Mail*:

The idea that this war is the last war and will end militarism is frankly flung aside. We are told that 'we must see to it that the utmost care shall be given to the children who, twenty years hence, may have to repel another German attack ... Shells and machine guns are the principal munitions of the present war, but infants are the munitions of the future peace'. We know how to translate that sentence. Shells and machine guns were said to be an insurance for peace before war broke out, but today they are the munitions of war. The infants of today are destined to be the first and chief munitions of the war which the *Daily Mail* sees as a possibility twenty years hence.

I call upon the collective motherhood of this nation and of the world to contemplate for one moment what this means. No war in the past has ever produced such casualty lists as the present war ... but all this falls into insignificance in comparison with the possibilities presented by the next war. Let submarine craft, air craft, and bomb craft develop during the next twenty years as they have developed in our lifetime, and we can scarcely imagine the wholesale murder and massacre which will ensue. If this thing is to go on, the human race as we know it today will be wiped off the surface of the planet. This is the immediate menace to our children and to our children's children.

This was a subject, then, to which our authors rightly attached a good deal of importance, and as already noted, the next publication in which they were involved was *Fecundity and Civilisation*.[99] This was issued under the name of the ubiquitous Adelyne More, but Philip Sargant Florence tells us that both he and his mother co-operated with Ogden in its production.[100] As the title and subtitle imply, it deals mainly with the adverse effects of a high birthrate on society in general and the position of women in particular. Mary Sargant Florence, in a letter to Ogden in June 1915, said that she considered the new work would be a 'big thing' and would 'arouse much more antagonism than *Militarism*'. Perhaps our judgement today would be to regret this emphasis as a diversion from the principal theme, especially in view of the very narrow line which divides these theories from those of the eugenics movement.

Nevertheless, the insights, ability and moral courage of these two writers and their unnamed collaborators deserve our attention and gratitude. Two more widely differing people could scarcely be imagined: Mary Sargant Florence, the dedicated artist, committing her resources and her time to suffragism and feminist pacifism, and C.K. Ogden, the Cambridge intellectual, waging all his life a campaign of words against injustice and intolerance of every kind. That they should co-operate to produce this call for social and international sanity is in itself a remarkable testimony to the strength of the anti-war movement of these years. The spark kindled by them, by Catherine Marshall and by many others, though barely perceptible at times, has not been extinguished and remains to be fanned by their spiritual heirs in a world even more threatened by antagonism and disunity. Again and again the words of *Militarism versus Feminism*, written in urgent response to a tragic world situation, strike us in the 1980s with their topicality and their warning. May they not have been written in vain.

Women and War[1]

Catherine E. Marshall

When within the course of a few short days last summer the nations of Europe (like climbers roped together on a dangerous precipice when the leader slips) were one after another engulfed in the great tragedy of war, I suppose the first thought in the minds of most of us women was a sense of shattering horror at the choice with which the men were confronted. The situation as it appeared to most British men was that either their country must fail to keep her pledged word, must turn a deaf ear to the cry of Belgium in her agony, or they — the whole manhood of the nation — must go forth to kill and be killed; to suffer, and, still worse, to inflict, all the horrors of war; to do violence to the whole spirit of civilisation, the whole teaching of Christianity.

Close upon this first thought, and the great flame of pity and tenderness it called forth in our hearts for the men who had this terrible choice to make, there came a crushing sense of our responsibility and guilt — the guilt of the peoples — in having permitted such a tragedy to come to pass. It is true that the peoples have not wanted war; but they have not willed peace. They have been content if their rulers have avoided *making war*; they have not insisted that they should, positively and constructively, *make peace* — make the conditions that promote mutual trust and co-operation instead of acquiescing in conditions that promote mutual suspicion and enmity. If the peoples had cared enough for peace they would have known no rest until they had established such relations between the civilised countries as would have made a disaster like the present war impossible. For the choice with which our men are faced today need not have been the only choice; the sacrifices each nation is making need not have been necessary sacrifices. Honour demands, truly, that a nation shall keep its word, that it shall not leave in the lurch a neighbour whom it had led to count on its support. But honour does *not* demand that destruction or bloodshed shall be the only means of fulfilling these obligations. It is only because we have neglected to provide other means that we found ourselves last August confronted with the choice between breaking our faith with our neighbour or violating the law of Christ and of human brotherhood.

And for this lack of will to peace, this acquiescence in conditions which made possible, if not inevitable, the cataclysm in which we are now involved, we women have realised at last that we share the responsibility; and in that fact lies, as I believe, the great hope for the future, the source from which the peace forces will be able to draw new motive-power. The mother-heart of womanhood has been stirred to its depths; and it is a womanhood whose sense of responsibility has been developed, whose mind has been educated, whose capacity for co-operation has been trained by the Women's Movement, with all that it has meant of awakening and enlightenment, and the widening of sympathy.

And what contribution has this awakened womanhood to offer for the solution of the great problems of reconstruction that the civilised world has got to face?

Women in all countries have proved the value of their service in relieving the suffering and mitigating the material evils caused by war; and the most valuable qualities they have brought to this work have been the qualities of imagination, of faith, of dauntless love; their habit of regarding people under all circumstances as human beings, and not merely as ciphers in an Army estimate or a Census return; their experience as mothers and as heads of households, in presiding over the mutual relations of the separate human units of which a family or a household is composed, adjusting the claims and needs of its various members, with their different temperaments, their different stages of growth, in such a way that each may develop all his powers to the full and use them for the common good of all. In some instances, women's very inexperience has been of value; it has made them refuse to be daunted by difficulties which to men, tired and discouraged by former failures, had appeared unsurmountable.

I believe that all these qualities are just as much needed for the work of creating a new social fabric as for the patching and mending of the existing fabric on which war has wrought such destruction. I believe that just as women can do much for the healing of the physical wounds which men are inflicting on one another, so they can do much also for the healing of the deeper and more disastrous spiritual wounds which nation is inflicting on nation. I believe that women, if they turn their minds in that direction, are more likely than men to find some other way of settling international disputes than by an appeal to force, partly because that is an appeal which is not open to them as women, and they have, therefore, never been accustomed to rely upon it. (It is interesting to trace the analogy between the position of women and that of the smaller nations in this respect.) I believe that the experience and habits of mind which women acquire as mothers of families and as heads of households might, if applied to a wider field, throw new light on the problems of the great human family of nations, and help to build up a better system of international relations which would make impossible the repetition of such a tragedy as that in which we are now involved.

But above all I believe that on women rests a large share of the responsibility for providing the motive-power which alone can make all these things possible, and without which the most perfect machine in the world will not work. And I believe that this motive-power is to be found in the deep horror of war which has entered for the first time into the soul of an organised women's movement. Women, thousands of individual women, have known that horror indeed only too well in the past; for war, to women, is pre-eminently an outrage on motherhood and all that motherhood means; the destruction of life and the breaking-up of homes is the undoing of women's work as life-givers and home-makers. But in former great wars there was not an organised women's move-ment to give expression to the passion of horror in the women's hearts, to be fired by it to co-operative action. Today there is such a women's movement, organised, articulate, in almost all the belligerent and most of the neutral countries. And I believe the great call to the women's movement, if we have ears to hear and the courage and faith and love enough to res-pond to it, is that we should face and visualise the full horrors of war, accepting our share of responsibility as those who might have helped, had we cared enough, to save the world from this tragedy.

I believe that this is the share which we, as women and non-combatants, are called upon to take in mak-ing this truly a 'war to end war', to 'put an end to militarism' — in ensuring that the sacrifices our men are making shall not have been made in vain.

Let us look steadfastly at war and the consequences of war, with our women's eyes — our mother's eyes — and tell the world what we see. Let us look honestly and courageously, 'les yeux bien ouverts, les yeux qui veulent voir',[2] shirking none of the pain and the horror, refusing to be blinded by glamour. (There is no glamour about the wrecked homes of Belgium and E. Prussia. If we succeed in carrying out our threat to stop food supplies from reaching Germany there will be no glamour for the women who see their children and their invalids and their old people dying of starvation.) We must not shut our eyes to any of the wickedness of it; we must let the pity and the shame of it enter deep into our hearts and rouse a passionate determination that these things shall never be again.

It is by this deliberate opening of our hearts to all the pain and suffering, this sharing in the sense of responsibility and sin, that even the simplest and humblest of us may attain the power and the wisdom to build up the new world of our dreams. This is the great truth taught in the legend of Parsifal, 'der reine Thor, durch Mitleid wissend'[3] — the pure-hearted fool who, through compassion, through sharing in the suffering and sin of the world, attained wisdom and understanding. It was not enough that he should see and pity physical suffering; he grieved over the swan he had killed, but he did not understand. It was not enough that he should see the repentance of another; he was permitted to witness the mystery of the Holy Grail and the agony of Amfortas, but still he did not understand; he looked on as a fool, blindly, from outside. It was only when he himself participated in the greatest suffering of all — the sense of sin — that enlightenment came. That sense entered his heart in an agonising flash; he knew, he understood.

41

From that moment his path lay clear before him. He went out to his task in the world, and he became worthy not only to receive and understand the mystery of the Grail, but to be its keeper, to administer its blessing to others.

Let us too seek this knowledge and understanding. Let us not try to escape any of the agony of remorse that it will bring; for out of that agony a new hope will be born, a new force will arise in the world. In this way, and I believe in this way only, can we truly follow in the steps of Him who came 'to bring light to them that walk in darkness and in the shadow of death, and to guide our feet into the way of peace'.

The Future of Women in Politics[1]

Catherine E. Marshall

The future of women in politics depends, more even than does the future of democracy itself, on whether the war results in the discrediting of militarism, or whether it leaves all the nations more militarist than they were before.

Conversely it is true that whether the civilised world does or does not surrender its soul to militarism will depend in no small measure on what place women are going to take in politics.

The militarist is one who believes in the supremacy of force, who justifies the use of power to compel submission to the desires of its possessor, without any further sanction than his own conviction that his desires be reasonable. In a state where the social order is based on the power to exercise force women must always go to the wall, just as in a community of nations in which force is the deciding factor in international differences the smaller nations must always go to the wall. Further, this theory of the supremacy of force, and the right of its possessors to use it to impose their will on others, tells in favour of those in possession of power of whatever kind, whether of wealth, or office, or political ascendancy. Those who have a monopoly of any of these things have the power to withhold them from those who have them not. The large nation can dominate the small one. The capitalist can exploit the worker. Men can continue to exclude women from the franchise to deny them economic and legal independence.

This war has revealed a new danger inherent in modern militarism. In former times the issue of a war depended very largely on the personal valour and skill of those engaged in it. In the present war success, according to the military critics, is bound to go ultimately to whichever side has the greatest resources in money and men, and uses those resources on the soundest business principles. It is simply a matter of counting heads and measuring the length of the purse. If that is so then the militarism of the future means not only a yet more enormous expenditure on armies and navies; it means also that the value of men or women will be reckoned according to their capacities as money-makers or breeding machines. This prospect is not an encouraging one for the workers or the women, or for those who are striving against commercialism and materialism for the higher ideals of human progress.

Men have hitherto accepted the dominance of force as inevitable. They have met force by force. They have believed that when radical changes are needed they can only be brought about by fighting; and there are certain things which mankind will always believe to be worth fighting for if they cannot be got in any other way. The chief of these is liberty.

Unfortunately the end is apt to cast a glamour over the means; and just as militarism — the belief in force — conduces to fighting, so does fighting conduce to militarism. Means which were resorted to with reluctance, as being the only means of obtaining a necessary end, become glorified in the process as things good in themselves. The mark of your militarist is that he would rather get what he wants by fighting than by any other way. He wants to force his enemy to yield, so that he may have him at his mercy and be able to impose what terms he chooses. I have heard trade unionists talk like this of trade union rights. I have heard socialists, who were ardent pacifists on international questions, talk like this of class warfare. I have heard suffragists talk like this of the struggle for sex equality. *They were all talking pure militarism —* they were all moved by the desire to dominate rather than to co-operate, to vanquish and humiliate the enemy rather than to convert him into a friend.

I am convinced that the future of women in politics depends largely on whether this attitude prevails in the peace settlement at the end of this war, and in the national as well as the international readjustments which will have to follow afterwards. The future of women in politics depends still more on whether the women in the different nations and the different classes identify themselves with this attitude, or whether they set themselves strenuously to oppose it, not by fighting or by any negative form of opposition, but by setting up a finer and more inspiring ideal in its place — the ideal of Right, instead of Might, of co-operation instead of conflict.

But how can women, with their lack of experience in business and in politics, hope to contribute anything practical to the solution of a problem of this kind, which means no less than the reorganisation of society on a new basis?

I believe that women's experience as mothers and heads of households has given them just the outlook on human affairs which is needed in this process of reconstruction. Nay, more; I believe that their relative inexperience in business and politics is in this matter an advantage. Women coming straight from their experience in the home to the consideration of national and international politics are likely to bring with them the standards and values of the home. And is not that just what we need? Do we not want the outlook that sees men as human beings, and politics as the business of adjusting human relations so that all shall have their rights, and opportunity for the free development of all their faculties in the service of the community as a whole?

From time immemorial a man has regarded his duty to his family as primarily a matter of getting for it the things that it wants. The women's duty has been first to give and nurture life, and secondly to transform for use the raw material brought in by the man, and distribute it according to the family's needs. His energies have been concentrated on getting, hers on giving. He brings in the game he has trapped or shot for food, she cooks and distributes it; he brings home the money he has earned in wages, she spends it on the various needs of the household; he builds the walls of a house, she transforms it into a home.

This accumulated experience has affected men's attitude towards one another in business, in politics, and in international relations. If you regard getting and holding as the chief business of life it is natural to regard your neighbours as rivals and competitors, whom you must fight and outwit. It is natural also to value men according to their power to get and to hold, or their usefulness in helping others to exercise this power.

The woman's point of view, applied to politics, would introduce a new valuation. We have become too much accustomed to talk of men as 'hands' in a factory, or 'heads' to be polled at an election; or as 'casualties' (!) by which to measure military success or failure. To a woman every man is a mother's son — not as her possession, but as her gift of great price which must not be wasted, her great adventure on which she has staked her all. This view involves a revaluation indeed, based not on power or on wealth but on humanity; not on getting but on giving; not on domination, but on service.

Then there is another way in which women's experience fits them peculiarly to help men in the reorganisation of international relations which we all hope will be one of the outcomes of this present war. Men's efforts to 'preserve peace' (as if you could preserve that which is not there!) have been directed mainly to preserving the status quo, to repressing any force that threatened to disturb the existing order. Now that is all very well for those who have all they want under the existing order, — for the British Empire, for the capitalist, for the party in power. But what about those who are not satisfied with things as they are? Surely the business of those who desire a real living peace is to find some means other than war by which the existing order can be changed to meet legitimate needs and changing conditions?

How could women help in this task? Would not their traditional conservatism be a hindrance rather than a help?

It is true that women are by instinct conservers — but of Life, not of the status quo; and life means inevitably growth and change, as all their experience has taught them. A mother is used to providing for the needs of a growing child. She does not say to the child: 'You must not grow, because I have made clothes for you of a certain size, and I do not want the trouble of altering them or making new ones'. The wise mother makes those clothes with tucks that can be easily let out; and when they can be let out no further she starts on a new garment so as to have it ready when needed. Always the *human need* is the first consideration, not the maintenance of things as they are at least cost to herself.

Democracies are growing children. Many nations

are still growing children. It is no use to say: 'You must not grow; you must put up with clothes that are too tight for you'. The function of statesmanship is to provide for the healthy growth and development of all the members of the human family.

There is yet a third task awaiting women in politics. I believe that the reaction after this war will give a tremendous impetus to the development of internationalism. The growing sense of common aims and needs among the workers of all nations will break down national barriers — unless militarism keeps them up. But the sense of common interests tells in other classes as well. They too will become increasingly conscious of bonds of union. Even the militarists of different countries will join hands if they see their common interests in danger. This will all tend to break down national antagonisms, but if class hatred takes their place we shall be no nearer the goal of human brotherhood. There will be little gained if we abolish international warfare only to set up warfare of another sort — a war which, even if armed force were not used, would bring in its train all the worst evils of war as we see it today; the same bitterness and violence, the same blinding of the combatants to all considerations except the necessity of beating the enemy; the same suffering of the innocent with the guilty; and the destruction of all that civilisation has laboured to build up.

Just as the common aims and needs of the workers cut across national barriers, so does the common motherhood of woman cut across national barriers and class barriers alike. We were all agreed, at the beginning of this war at any rate, in thinking that if the international solidarity of the workers had been more fully developed and firmly established this war could not have taken place. They would have insisted that some other and saner way than war must be found for settling the issues at stake. Can the solidarity of women be developed in such a way as to strengthen this movement towards internationalism, and at the same time to help to find some other way than class war for bringing about the changes necessary in our social structure? Granted the insight and the will to do this, can we act? Are we going to be given a direct voice in politics? Are we going to be given it *in time*?

In this country that rests largely with the Labour Party. Will they demand the introduction of a Franchise Bill immediately after the war is over, and will they insist that in that Bill Woman Suffrage on a basis that will enfranchise the working mother must be included and must be retained in the Bill in all its stages?[2] They will be tempted by every ruse, and by every appeal to apparent self-interest, to agree to leave the women out — to get manhood suffrage firmly established first and *then* work for the inclusion of women. The opponents of democracy know well that once the men's franchise is complete it will be far easier to keep women out. They will not dare to refuse the men, but they will feel it a comparatively easy matter to exclude women — just as women have been excluded from public houses during certain hours to give the appearance of temperance reform, whilst leaving to the trade their most paying customers, the men.

Women will enter increasingly into all branches of industry, not only now, but after the war. It will be to the interests of those who want to exploit the working classes to keep women unenfranchised, even if that is not possible in the case of the men. Are the men going to allow it?

We could do much if we had the power which the vote brings. We can do something without it. As I write, a new women's organisation is being born, to be

51

called the Women's International League, which will have as its object 'to establish the principles of Right rather than Might, and co-operation rather than conflict, in national and international affairs, and for this purpose to work for (1) the development of the ideals underlying modern democracy in the interests of constructive peace, and (2) the emancipation of women and the protection of their interests, including their admission to the Parliamentary franchise, their admission to National and International Councils, and the establishment of their economic independence and legal freedom'.

The formation of this League, and of similar organisations in other countries, is the outcome of the Women's International Congress held at The Hague last April, under the presidency of Miss Jane Addams, of Hull House, Chicago. That Congress marked the opening of a new chapter in the Women's Movement, and in the unfolding of that chapter lies, as I believe, the great hope for the future of women in politics.

Militarism versus Feminism

An Enquiry and a Policy Demonstrating
that Militarism Involves the
Subjection of Women

C.K. Ogden and Mary Sargant Florence

Note

The following pages, in so far as they do not deal with purely historical questions, look forward to a time when the Women's Movement will once more be able calmly to take stock of its position. As regards the nations now at war, effective action on the lines suggested is hardly to be expected at present; but in neutral countries the situation is already being seriously faced. Apart from the Dutch invitation for an International Congress, the Women's Peace Movement in the USA, under the presidency of Miss Jane Addams, is winning the unanimous support of American suffragists, who realise the extent to which their own cause is threatened by the European situation.

All who are interested in the practical problems of organisation thus raised will find a full and reliable record in *Jus Suffragii* which, as the organ of the International Suffrage Alliance, has proved itself invaluable as a source of information since the events of August, 1914. Portions of the present investigation have already appeared in its columns, and in those of the *Common Cause* and the *Cambridge Magazine*, and are here reproduced by kind permission of the Editors. As stated on page 63 it is hoped that a larger volume may later take the place of this necessarily brief survey, and anyone willing to supply further evidence or suggestions, or to point out errors, is earnestly invited to communicate with the authors, c/o Messrs. Allen and Unwin.[1]

Introduction

It is hard indeed, at a time like the present, to detach oneself even for a moment from the duties which the common danger has imposed on us all — men and women in every country. But, sooner or later, our attitude to certain fundamental questions must be decided, lest the critical moment come upon us unprepared. Every movement that stands for progress raises such questions, and none is more important than the future of the women's movement in relation to war and militarism. Will — or should — its course be modified in the light of recent events? It is hardly too early to discuss this question, for the advocates of militarism are already busy in our midst, and it is easy to take a wrong turning or a short view. Opinions within the movement are divided. Yet it seems probable that there would be less disagreement if once the results of militarism were clearly understood.

We are faced by issues on which it seems not improbable that the ideals of most men are different from those of most women. The difference has usually been obscured in feminist propaganda: the argument so often has to run, and quite truly, that on the majority of questions there will be no great split of society into two halves, the men wanting one thing

55

and the women another. But militarism, as such, raises different problems.

For feminism history has only one message on the question of war, and it is this:

Militarism has been the curse of women, as women, from the first dawn of social life. Owing to the turmoil in which it has kept every tribe and every nation almost without exception, mankind has seldom been able to pause for a moment to set social affairs in order — and the first and most crying reform has ever been the condition of woman. Violence at home, violence abroad; violence between individuals, between classes, between nations, between religions; violence between man and woman: *this it is which, more than all other influences, has prevented the voice of woman being heard in public affairs until almost yesterday.* War has created *slavery* with its degrading results for women, and its double standard of morality from which we are not yet completely free: war, and the consequent enslavement of women, has been the main inducement to *polygamy*, with its conception of women as property, and its debasement of love to physical enjoyment: war has engendered and perpetuated that dominance of man as a military animal which has pervaded every social institution from *Parliament* downwards. In war man alone rules: when war is over man does not surrender his privileges. Militarist ethics have perverted the peaceful and individualising tendencies of *industry* to which woman owes so much. Industry has united with competition to produce industrial warfare: commerce has combined with imperialism for the capture of markets and the exploitation of the lower races. Militarism has ruined *education* with its traditions of discipline and its conception of history. Militarism has even left its blighting imprint on *religion* — on Mohammedanism the religion of conquest with its depreciation of woman;

on the religion of the Prince of Peace, so that the churches can say what they are not ashamed to say today. War, and the fear of war, has kept woman in perpetual subjection, making it her chief duty to exhaust all her faculties in the ceaseless production of children that nations might have the warriors needed for aggression or defence. She must not have any real education — for the warrior alone required knowledge and independence; she must not have a voice in the affairs of the nation, for war and preparation for war were so fundamental in the life of nations that woman, with her silly humanitarianism, must not be allowed to meddle therewith! And so war, which the influence of women alone might have prevented, was used as the main argument against enfranchisement, as it had been the main barrier to emancipation in the past. The circle is complete.

War, militarism, imperialism; in every form they have proved her undoing, and yet women hesitate today on which side to throw their influence! Over and over again the greatest statesmen have said that peace was utopian *only because public opinion was not ready for it*; and no one has said it more emphatically than Sir Edward Grey.[2] But who is to create the new public opinion? Have women no better answer than hatred or despair? Over and over again Suffragists have seen that it was from militarists that their ideals met with the most bitter opposition. They have never been tired of pointing to the baleful influence on our social life of ex-viceroys and of men accustomed to the military despotism of the East. Is it purely by chance that it is the countries which, by position or circumstances, have been most free from military domination and constant preparation for war that have felt able to listen to the demands of women? The United States, New Zealand, Norway, Finland, Iceland, and the rest — they are countries in which war plays but a small part. The conscriptionist countries, on the other hand, have always looked askance at women's claims, and who has not heard German women complain 'It's all very well for you to talk, but you don't know what it means to live in a country where everything is secondary to the training of the warrior male'? On February 5th, Mr Cloudesley Brereton wrote in the *Common Cause*, 'Germany stands forth as the chief exponent of the patriarchal conception.'[3] But, and let us not be led astray, only as the *chief* exponent; and from her faults let us learn. All Europe, as we show in Chapter III, is constantly menaced by similar tendencies. The Bernhardis of all nations are the danger; and, incidentally, we may note the following in the *Fortnightly* for January, 1915:

Later, I heard from the Countess that women were not much higher than the 'four-footed animal kingdom' for Bernhardi; that he loudly contradicted his wife, even at hotel tables when they travelled together; that he always walked ahead in the streets; and pushed past her or even other ladies (if strangers to him) in order to go first through a doorway.[4]

It is hard to write without danger of misrepresentation, and it is especially important to make it clear that nothing is here implied as regards *individuals*. As far as our argument goes the majority of men who compose the armies of Europe at the present moment might be ardent supporters of women's rights! *The indictment is against militarism*. Since the war broke out every woman's paper has been full of complaints as to the way in which women have been treated — quite apart from atrocities and sufferings, and the breakdown of the theory that women are 'protected,' so admirably exposed in the *Englishwoman*, January 1915.[5]

Yet war does but bring out tendencies suppressed in times of peace — the latent legacies of previous wars — and throughout history, as we show in Chapters II and III, it is in warlike ages and in warlike countries that women have fared worst. The age of mother-right, of which we hear so much today, was an age of peace, of agricultural communities whose women were not yet reduced to the subjection of the fighting patriarchal era which followed, and which with its organisation and traditions has survived even unto this day. Amongst primitive peoples, it is where peaceable conditions prevail that social and domestic arrangements accord to women the greatest liberty. The same is true of ancient Egypt, as Mrs Hartley[6] and others have shown. In Greece, the woman's movement (so badly needed in the Athens of Aristophanes) had already become the butt of the comedian when the warlike ambitions of Macedonia gave the death-blow to every effort of social reform. In a Rome worn out by ceaseless fighting, women were slowly attaining influence and liberty when the inroads of the barbarians again dashed their hopes to the ground. For centuries the battling hordes moved to and fro, and every forward movement amongst women had to contend in addition with the patriarchal system of marriage prescribed by the militarist legislators of the Old Testament, whose influence was now embedded in Christianity. And in modern times it has been the same, until in countries where the din of battle was no longer heard, and weapons of defence could at length be discarded in civil life, woman as woman dared to claim a share in directing those social affairs which concerned her so nearly.

For fifty years Great Britain had rested in peace at home after the exhaustion of the Napoleonic Wars, when John Stuart Mill first gave adequate expression to the murmurings of the centuries.[7] Since then the movement has gathered impetus day by day; but side by side with it militarism and imperialism have also raised their head. And so far militarism has prevailed! Its latest triumphs are now exposed even to the naked eye! Nor is the process merely unconscious. We have but to remember the ex-viceroys mentioned above. We have but to think of the effect on women of the Code Napoleon, the foundation of legislation in Latin countries, to see how the arch-militarist of modern Europe deliberately worked with military ends in view to subject and degrade women in social life. Consider the record of Mohammedanism in India; consider the blood-drenched past of China, with its foot-bound millions; consider Japan today — where are the New Women finding their chief opponents? And soon America too may realise to her cost the meaning of that military influence which her suffragists are suddenly straining every nerve to overcome. To the crowning example of modern Burma we have devoted a separate chapter. Is there any exception in the world's history? And if some apparent exception should present itself, would anyone challenge the main contention, neglected though it has been by suffragists in the past? In vain will England have fought against militarism today if, when the moment comes for diverting our national energies from the single task which now confronts us, women, who must stand apart from the conflict but suffer none the less, neglect an opportunity which may not occur again for centuries of directing public opinion satiated, as it will be, with the horrors of war, but impotent to escape for lack of vision.

To sum up: one of the possible, even probable consequences of this war will be an increase in the power of militarism, not only in the nations now fighting, but also in neutral countries overcome by the epidemic of international distrust. The only antidote to developments so inimical to women is the existence of an organised body of public opinion, fully conscious both of the great social ideals which the settlement might serve to promote and of the disastrous retrogression which would result from the establishment of an armed peace more threatening even than that of which this war was the outcome. The greatest hope for the formation of such a public opinion lies in the suffrage organisations whose aims and aspirations would be frustrated by the victory of the advocates of armaments and conscription. Men, as men, are powerless to move. Here is the prerogative of woman. Let her now take the lead. Already in America the most prominent feminist speakers and writers have recognised both the danger and the remedy.[8] When their programme is ripe, will the women of Europe be ready to carry it through? Will they, in making their decision, forget the lesson of history? Militarism has been their curse for centuries; its ideals have ever stood in the way of women's rights. Militarism will not change in the future. It must always produce an androcentric society, a society where the moral and social position of women is that of an essentially servile and subordinate section of the community. *In each single nation, taken for itself, men will be able to make a really good case for militarism, if the movement to educate public opinion does not become international.* For this reason above all others, it is the duty as well as the obvious interest of women to make clear their views with no uncertain voice. All other international bonds have been burst asunder by the war. Science, labour, religion, all have failed; but that silent half of humanity, permanently non-combatant, on whom the horrors of war fall with equal severity in all nations alike, bringing to all the same sorrows and the same sufferings, may through these very sorrows and sufferings find a new and real bond of unity for

61

the redemption and regeneration of the civilised world. Here at last it is clear that the higher ideals and aspirations of women coincide with the future welfare of the whole of humanity. In them is the hope of man.

Chapter I

A Land of Peace

'A married Burmese woman is much more independent than any European, even in the most advanced states.' − Sir J.G. Scott[9]

It will be the object of the following pages to show how the subjection of women, both now and in past ages, is essentially due to militarism, to the prevalence of war, and to the institutions and customs which are the legacies of war. In order the more strongly to emphasise this contention we have first selected the one country in the world in which at the present time women admittedly live as the equals of men, and where this equality is part of the traditions of the people. By showing that these advantages are essentially due to peace, and to the absence of martial institutions and customs, we shall also have done much to establish and illustrate our main proposition.

The example of Burma to which we are referring is all the more striking in view of the degraded position of women in the East as a whole − a degradation which if space allowed* could in every case be traced

---

* It is hoped that the present studies may be followed in due course by a larger volume, where the evidence for much that must necessarily be omitted here will be fully adduced.

directly to the influence of militarism or the reign of violence and bloodshed, which still prevails. In India, in China, and in Japan — the records of war are everywhere the same, and everywhere the desperate position of women is only too evident, as readers of Mrs Chapman Catt's[10] report to the International Suffrage Alliance in 1913 will be aware. The one exception is Burma. 'The freest women in Asia,' said Mrs Catt, 'are the Burmese. In that land rights for men and women are practically equal.' And the same view is expressed by the Burmese lady who wrote (in *Buddhism*, September, 1903):

'I have travelled in various countries, in West and East alike; have seen something of the lives the women of those countries lead; have heard something of their sorrows, of their ambitions, of their desires. And there is one thing I know, better than aught else in life — that I would sooner be a Burmese woman than one of any other land; sooner live the sweet and happy life of the Burmese village girl than that of the proudest nation of the West.'

And to what does she attribute this freedom?

'For myself I think that the secret of our happiness lies in our devotion to our beautiful Religion.'

But we can say more than this; though first of all we must understand something of the religion to which M.M. Hla Oung here refers. We must go back to the days when Gautama the Buddha dwelt in a little kingdom in the north-east of India.

No Buddha was he in those days: only a Prince, the Sakya Prince, Siddartha Gautama. He was strong, we are told, he was handsome and a famous athlete. A wife had he still and fair women to dance before him, and a joyful son withal. His future was full of all power, might, majesty, and dominion; and his father looked forward to the time when he should become a leader of armies, should lead his subjects against the

64

neighbouring kings, and in time create for himself a world-wide Empire.

Then it came to pass that on a day the Prince saw a Dead Man, that he learnt of death and suffering, that he saw the mystery of life, and saw too the vanity of Empire for which men murder one another. Straightway he sought for the laws that should lead mankind to the Great Peace.

Straightway the Prince Gautama forsook his dancing women, forsook his three palaces, the palace for the time of rains, the palace for the flower time and the palace for the fruit time. He forsook his wife and his son — that the wives and the sons of other men might have Peace. He the supreme Pessimist! He whose Optimism saw that the world might be ruled by righteousness, that the world might cease from strife and from the sin of battles, and might be at Peace with itself.

And the world — did it learn his wisdom? Once. Nearly.

The Ascendancy of Women

A few years ago an Englishman who knew the East, as few Europeans have known it, gave to the Western world an interpretation of the life and thought of an Eastern country which made Europe feel that here was something new and strange. 'I wanted,' he said, 'to write only what the Burmese themselves thought'; and the result was that for a moment the barrier which separates East and West seemed to be broken down.

The veil was lifted, and we saw the happiest people in the world; without nobles, without landowners, without bankers, without merchants. A people enamoured of freedom, a people amongst whom all is open, a people where all men are brothers. The

Burman does not care to be rich; he has learnt to despise wealth. He is overflowing with charity. He wants and he has love and companionship, fresh air and sunshine, and the great thoughts that come to you in the forest. He wants friends, he wants sympathy, he wants the joy of children. He believes that happiness is the best of all things. As we read of him we can breathe quietly in sheer delight; for here is he who toils hard and who is poor, but to whom life is one great festival, longer and larger than those wherein his joy is publicly celebrated.

'When you see the Burmese at their festivals, speeding the hours with song and dance and merriment, when you see the pleasure they take in bright clothes, in gaiety of demeanour, in the pleasanter things of life, you will laugh too.'

And what of the women?

In Burma women have equal rights with men. They are free, they have the same rights to property, they have equal opportunities for work. They have succeeded in imposing on the people generally many ideas which elsewhere are confined to the women alone.

What ideas are these? They are those for which the Prince Gautama forsook his wife and his son that the world might learn the law of peace.

That the command of the Buddhist faith over the Burmese people is due to the ascendancy of the women and women's ideas is very clear.

Again we ask. How was this possible? And a third time the answer comes without qualification. It is due to peace, to freedom from war.

The ascendancy of women was due to the secluded life the nation lived.

We have put three questions, and all of them we have been able to answer in the very words of the author of those two great interpretations of Eastern life *The Soul of a People* and *A People at School*.[11] Let us learn from Mr Fielding Hall yet a little more of this strange people, and let us also learn how they are to be purged of their misguided follies.

A Freedom Unknown Elsewhere

First of all as to the ultimate cause of Burmese happiness. There can be no doubt about it. We are told so again in other words, 'In Burma here, living their sheltered lives, never forced back by the rude blasts of an invading world, women gained a great ascendancy. They assumed a freedom unknown elsewhere.' This freedom and this ascendancy, possible only in the absence of war, the women turned to good account. The Buddha had taught the law of Happiness, had shown the way to the Great Peace — the Peace of the Soul; and his religion told that the Peace of the Soul was not possible if man should murder man in war. 'Its tenets and beliefs are women's tenets; they come easily to women's hearts, who believe by nature in the milder virtues; religion such as Buddhism is to them an evident truth.'

And the evident truth is this, 'Thou shalt take no life.' There is no exception to that at all, not even to a patriot fighting for his country. 'Thou shalt not take the life of even him who is the enemy of the king and nation.' If a man goes to the monks they can but say, 'See the law, there is no good thing but peace; no sin but the strife of war.' Buddhism, we learn, never bent to popular opinion, never made itself a tool in the hands of worldly fashion.

No soldier could be a true Buddhist; no nation of Buddhists could be good soldiers. No ravished country has ever borne witness to the prowess of the followers of the Buddha; no murdered men have poured out their blood on their hearthstones killed in his name; no ruined women have cursed his name to high Heaven. No psalm has been sung in his temples to honour the warrior that taketh the foeman's children and dasheth them against the stones. Never has the Sun stood still that his people might not cease from the slaughtering of their enemies. He was the preacher of the Great Peace, of love, of charity, of compassion; and so clear is his teaching that it can never be misunderstood.

Yet the Burmese are like other men. They are but men, and men fight. They have been surrounded by warlike tribes: they have been led astray by ambitious kings: and in their wars they have even been cruel — like other nations. They have fought in Siam, in Assam, and in Pegu: and above all they have fought against the English. But they have never fought in the name of their faith. The Burman can be very brave. When he is wantonly attacked, sometimes the animal within him leaps out and he cannot suppress his human bravery. But he sins with his eyes open; he makes no excuses; he looks for no reward. The foeman's sword is no key to open to him the gates of Paradise; his monks do not come near to close his dying eyes with murmurs of the justice of his cause. Yes, he can be very brave. In Buddhism there is no fear of death.

The Miracle of Miracles

But the instinct of pugnacity has been tamed; the miracle has been performed. Let us once more quote verbally that there may be no mistake:

His instincts make him like hunting, lead him to kill noxious beasts and reptiles. But in every home the mother and wife enforce the prohibition against taking life.

This influence of women is surely the most precious and wonderful thing in history, and the picture of Burmese women, of women in the only country which has ever known the meaning of peace, is indeed one at which we may pause. Peace has meant everything to them. They knew no limits but their own disinclination, and their weaknesses were little handicap to them. They came and went as freely as the men did, seeking for escort only where there were dangers to be feared, wild beasts or floods; of men they had little fear. The dangers that await women elsewhere when alone in fields or forests were small in Burma. The men respected the women, and the latter could defend themselves. The result is that she has been bound by no ties, and had no frozen ideals of a long dead past, no hoary patriarchal traditions, held up to her as eternal copies. She has looked after herself, and the marks of this freedom and of this development are seen everywhere. Thus the administration of the law in all that concerns sex is the same for man and woman; marriage, inheritance, divorce, criminal law — all alike show no partiality. Nor is it surprising to learn how strange it is, talking to Burmese girls, to see how much they know and understand of the world about them. It is to them no great mystery, full of unimaginable good and evil, but 'a world that they are learning to understand, and where good and evil are never unmixed.' They have no 'accomplishments,' for very few Burmese girls are left with superfluous time on their hands. And of the children we are told 'they grow up little merry naked things, sprawling in the dust of the gardens, sleeping in the sun with their arms round the village dogs, very sedate, very humorous, very rarely crying.'

If this were all we might merely close with the remark, 'Very imaginative, very pretty,' and forget about it as soon as possible in order to be free to subscribe to some Burmese Mission. But that is not quite all; for there is the future to consider.

We have quoted Mr Fielding Hall. We are aware that some writers disagree with him — but whether or no his picture be accurate, it is important to discover the steps which so enlightened and sympathetic a writer advocates in order to preserve for the world this wonderful social heritage — this model for the advocates of women's rights in all lands. It may be that he has idealised the Burmese. That is no concern of ours. He has at least given us an ideal which they may strive to attain if they have in fact failed to reach it. What are the author's own views for the future? They are all the more significant because Mr Hall was recently a government official, and went through the Burmese war, obtaining as Political Officer, 1887—91, a medal and two clasps. His opinion must carry considerable weight, and to judge from his writings will be decidedly more liberal than that of most administrators and officials in the East. Indeed, we may gather this from a discussion of the doctrine of peace set forth above with a soldier friend. 'What is the use,' asks the friend, 'of this religion that we see so many signs of? What do these monks do? I never see them in a fight, never hear that they are doing anything to organise the people. What is the use of Buddhism?' He was a brilliant soldier, comments Mr Hall, and a religion was to him a sword, a thing to fight with. That was one of the first uses of a religion. He knew nothing of Buddhism; he cared to know nothing but whether it would fight. If so it was a good religion in its way. If not, then not.

So much for the opinion of the soldier. Now for the administrator. He has described the country. He has described its ideal — the Great Peace. Into this country, as he tells us, has come the British Government with sword and rifle preaching another faith. How it came does not concern us directly. It is a terrible tale. Let us remain silent. The religion of Burma delivers the country bound to its enemies. The conquest was not difficult. The Burmese were goaded to sin against their faith and offered some small resistance. 'But today,' says Mr Hall, 'the laws are ours, the power, the authority. We govern for our own objects, and we govern in our own way. Our whole presence here is against their desires.'

Great Britain has power to do what she will. She can encourage or destroy the faith that has made for peace. She can allow the capitalist system to undermine the position of women, or she can prevent it from doing so. What is being done? What ought to be done? The question is of interest to women as well as to men. *She that hath an ear to hear let her hear.*

What's Wrong With the Burmese?

There are two things, we are told, wrong with the Burmese:

1. They have not learnt the art of fighting.
2. They have not learnt that the world is a man's world.

Therefore —

1. The men must be taught to fight.
   'I can imagine nothing that could do the Burmese so much good as to have a regiment of their own to distinguish itself in our wars. It would open their eyes to new views of life.' *A People at School* p. 264.
2. The women must surrender their liberty in the interests of man.

'It has never been good for women to be too independent.'

'It improves a man to have to work for his wife; it makes a man of him.' *A People at School* p. 266.

We may open our eyes in amazement and horror: but there it is. All that is good in Burma comes from its religion of peace and from the equality of man and woman. But they must be taught that 'the world is a man's world.' They have not realised the great truth. Why?

'Their Faith stands in the way, and their Women.'

Such are Mr Hall's words: and the arguments by which he establishes his conclusions are most instructive.

A Thousand Years Behind Us!

First of all as to the faith which stands in the way. That is to be cured not by another faith but by war. When the missionaries from Europe tell the Burmese Buddhist that our success is due to our faith, the Burmese Buddhist laughs. He reads the Sermon on the Mount and reflects. He turns upon the missionary and says, 'Your faith denounces war, but you attack and subject us; your faith denounces riches but you pursue them all day long; your faith preaches humility, but there are none so proud as you. You succeed because you do *not* believe, not because you do.'

But what the Burman wants is, Mr Hall thinks, not Christianity or any other faith. He already has too much faith. He has been nursed and cosseted and preached at too much. He must get up and fight. 'He must throw off his swaddling bands of faith and find the natural fighter underneath. He must learn to be

72

savage if necessary, to destroy, to hurt and push aside without scruple. He must learn to be a man.'

No wonder Mr Hall could write that amazing sentence — 'It must never be forgotten that their civilisation is relatively a thousand years behind ours.' Perhaps it will be some consolation to them to observe how much the present war will throw us back. For hitherto they had failed to realise the futility of peace. The eternal verity that the world belongs to the strongest, the Burmese had forgotten. 'In their great valley between the mountain ranges and the sea, free from all invaders, with a kindly earth yielding food in ample quantities, it had fallen into the second place. The manly nature had sunk into disrepute, rusted by disuse, unsharpened by the clash with the weapons of others.' Poor misguided creatures, they valued their ideal of peace too high. They had made a religion thereof to establish it the more securely; 'Religion,' says Mr Hall, 'which is true only when second to the truths of life, was exalted into the first place. The greater truth may be when rightly understood, the more false its falsehood when it is misplaced. And in Burma Buddhism had risen to that place.'

Men are Men and Women are Women!

But foul as are the horrors of peace, the high position of women has had even more disastrous results. We have seen how the women repressed the natural fighting propensities of the males. So sheepish did men become under this regime that their instincts no longer served them in the choice of good and evil. 'That hunting was a grand and brave sport, that war was a pleasure and a glory never occurred to them.'

Yet strange to tell 'the men are not effeminate.' Rather, they are naturally courageous; and when roused by the British invasion they fought long and bravely. No, it is on other grounds that they must be taught to fight and introduced to the glories of war. It is on other grounds that women must surrender their liberty. Hear, O ye nations:

Men are Men and Women are Women!

This great truth and its inevitable consequences are set forth as follows. 'What man can do best it is best he should do. If it brings him great power, greater authority, it also gives him greater responsibility. Such is best for both.' It may, we are told, be pleasant for a girl to be the equal heiress of her brother. But it is not the way to make the best either of law or money. Nor does it make the best men or women. It is not good for a man to be feminised. It is not good for him to feel that he has no greater right than a woman, for he immediately and rightly infers that he has no greater responsibilities. It is not good for him to have woman's ideals. A woman may say, 'I am afraid.' It is her right. Courage is not a virtue that the world wants from woman. But for a man to be a coward and to openly confess and without shame that he is so is a sad thing. Now the Burmese generally are no cowards. They are naturally courageous. Yes, here we have it. It is the business of a man to fight, 'and an army keeps alive the cult of bravery and discipline, of self-denial, of cohesion.' Today, alas 'there is no army at all . . . Even if a man be brave now and energetic, he has no scope for showing his qualities. To see a brave soldier rise to honour, to hear and see brave deeds done by one's own people is more ennobling to a nation than any wealth or any learning. The Burmese in their sheltered valleys learnt this virtue very little; they have now none of it. It is a loss. I do not see how a people worth anything can be made without it.' The

74

miserable Burmese think only of peace, of friendship, of joy, of sunshine and of happiness: they refuse to fight properly: 'The regiments we have tried to raise have not succeeded. It is a pity. They may, however, succeed later. I can imagine nothing that could do the Burmese so much good as to have a regiment of their men distinguish itself in our wars. It would open their eyes to new views of life. But their faith stands in their way, and their women.'

It was worth repeating this considered recommendation in order to be quite sure of the real meaning of Mr Hall's proposals. Militarism in the East is a terrible thing. Think of the circular memorandum (quoted on pp. 17–19 of *The Queen's Daughters in India*)[12] sent to all the cantonments of India by Quartermaster-General Chapman in the name of the then Commander-in-Chief of the Indian Army (Lord Roberts), and beginning 'In the regimental bazaars (i.e. in the chalka or brothel) it is necessary to have a sufficient number of women, to take care that they are sufficiently attractive, etc.' Think of the hideous record of militarism revealed in the article 'Militarism, Prostitution and Disease,' in the *Shield* for January 1915. To all this Burma is to be exposed for the good of its soul!

We have, however, thus reached the conclusion we desired: and, in conformity with the new ideal, the Burmese are already being taught to kill animals. War itself will soon cure them of their peaceful habits. 'What the surgeon's knife is to the diseased body that is the soldier's sword to the diseased nations.'

By Spear and Sword

Again we must remember 'the world is not a hospital but a battlefield. The gospel of progress, of knowledge, of happiness ... is taught not by book and sermon but by spear and sword.' 'Buddhism with its feminine ideals and its cult of peace, was never fitted to be leader of a race.' We have seen the utter inadequacy of a religion that makes light of war. 'To declare, as Buddhism does, that bravery is of no account; to say to them, as the women did, you are no better and no more than we are, and should have the same code of life; could anything be worse?' It is terrible: but ethnology here comes to our aid. 'Men and women are not sufficiently differentiated yet in Burma. It is the mark of a young race. Ethnologists tell us that. In the earliest people the difference was very slight. As a race grows older the difference increases.' So no doubt they will grow out of their absurd habits. In time they may even take to war, and learn their deficiencies from the glorious history of Europe.

Down, Down, Down — Hurrah!

In the meantime there is every hope that women will rapidly be reduced to the condition of their sisters elsewhere in the East. An alien denomination and its influences are already threatening their position in many ways. Their means of livelihood is being taken from them. Hitherto they have been independent and powerful because they could live by their own efforts. Today home industries are being killed as they have already been killed in Europe, and European institutions and methods are taking their place. 'In Rangoon the large English stores are undermining the Bazaars where the women used to earn an independent livelihood.' Everywhere trade 'is falling into stronger hands, as elsewhere in the world.' Nothing is being done to counteract these tendencies. Nor should anything be done. Indeed we are told it is absolutely essential 'that the laws of marriage and inheritance must be modified. All the changes are to the detriment of the position of the woman as it now stands.'

Down, down, she goes: and Mr Hall faces her degradation with complete equanimity.

'With her power of independence will disappear her free-will and her influence. When she is dependent on her husband she can no longer dictate to him. When he feeds her, she is no longer able to make her voice as loud as his is. It is inevitable that she should retire ... The nations who succeed are not the feminine nations, but the masculine. Women's influence is good provided it does not go too far. Yet it has done so here. It has been bad for the man, bad too for the woman. It has never been good for women to be too independent, it has robbed them of many of their virtues. It has never been good for men to feel that their women-folk were independent of their help. It improves a man to have to work for his wife and family, it makes a man of him. It is demoralising for both if the woman can keep herself and if necessary her husband too.'

Why is it demoralising? Because the world is a man's world, and for no other reason! Burmese women must understand the new conditions. They must surrender their liberty in the interests of men. In return, however, they will receive safety, and the blessing of dependence. They will be able to rely upon their fathers, their husbands, their sons, more than they do now, and if the men are to have more power they must be ready to accept more responsibility. Women rule us in our youth, and in our age. But in the prime of life, it is the men who lead. The Burmese, as we have seen, have the characteristics which (as ethnologists tell us) belong to a young nation. And happily for them they are also a rising

77

nation. 'It is the mark of rising nations that men control and women are not seen.'

East and West

There have been many causes which have contributed to the degradation or subjection of woman in the past, but the most fundamental and universal of all are war and martial ideals. Some proof of this we have offered above, and the statement holds of Europe at the present time no less than of earlier centuries. The connection has sometimes been obscured but it is always there; in Burma its reality is revealed in the clearest form. Today a great Empire is fighting for its existence; fighting, it claims, for liberty. For fifty years the women within that Empire have struggled for their liberty — and but few have yet attained it. The future of their cause is bound up with the future of militarism which has dominated the world in the past. Soon peace will come again, and with peace a parting of the ways: on the one side those who would perpetuate the old militarism and international pugnacity: on the other side the advocates of co-operation, with whom will be found the true followers of Christ not less than the disciples of Gautama. On which side will the women be found who now gaze helplessly at the slaughter, and whose own ideals, though they may not realise it, hang in the balance? The example and possible fate of Burma may not be without value to those whose minds are not yet made up; for apart from the lesson of that example it is on the decision and future of the women's movement in Europe and America that the future of women, not only in Burma but in the East generally, now largely depends.

When the Western world has settled its present differences, there is yet one more danger to face. East is East and West is West; but how many are striving to bring them together? Alliances and Governments alone can do but little here: often they may work directly, if unwittingly, towards further disunion. Knowledge, understanding and sympathy are necessary, and above all public opinion. Our story has shewn that even with the best of intentions men are not likely of their own accord to realise in which direction progress lies! At the moment perhaps little can be done. But sooner or later an attempt will have to be made to form this public opinion: indeed, whilst these pages were passing through the press Sir William Wedderburn in a letter to the *New Statesman*[13] came forward to advocate the immediate entry of women into this wide field of reconciliation and understanding which he contended was closed to the official male. Women have done much in the past to modify the ideals of men. It is perhaps not unreasonable to hope that in this matter, where their interests are so clearly identical all the world over and so clearly harmonise with those of civilisation as a whole, their united and conscious efforts might succeed where all else would fail.

Let us, however, return from this larger question, and from the contemplation of the advantages which peace can confer, to the study of the record of militarism as it is revealed in history.

Chapter II

The Lesson of History — I

'Nothing could be more timely in 1915 than insistence on the lesson that Militarism involves the Subjection of Women.' — Mrs H.M. Swanwick

Though the effects of militarism have been the same in East and West alike as far as women are concerned, in what follows we may most profitably concentrate our attention on the problems of Europe alone, which affect the immediate future more nearly. And, furthermore, it will be well to begin at the beginning.

Not many years ago when the word 'matriarchy' came into popular use it was often assumed that in primitive times women enjoyed a freedom and a superiority which in a later age she lost. The cry was thus at once raised by suffragists that so far from the present subjection of women being natural and necessary, history shows on the contrary that male despotism is a comparatively late growth; a more or less casual excrescence with little foundation in natural tendency other than the determination of man to retain what chance has cast in his way. Hence right up to the outbreak of the war all attention was concentrated on the vote, the symbol of political equality, and at times when suffrage propaganda flagged little else seemed worth attention.

Such a view, in spite of all the admitted evidence against it, is still widely held, and has probably contributed not a little to the failure of so many women to grasp the significance for their cause of the events of 1914 and the national rivalries which led up to those events. But it is a view which is both erroneous and unnecessarily unjust to men. It is absolutely essential to effective action in the future that the historical development of the movement should be clearly understood; and as a first step towards such an understanding it cannot be too frequently pointed out (as Professor Hobhouse, above all others, has now so clearly demonstrated) that an imagined *matriarchy*, or rule of the mother, has nothing whatever to do with the *mother-right* which does, as a matter of fact, exist in primitive society. Though the wife remains a member of her own family; though the children take the mother's name, and belong to her; though property passes in the mother's name, or even to her — all this leaves it 'perfectly possible for the position of women to be as low as the greatest misogynist could desire.'[14] In a word, it is now a matter of almost universal agreement among sociologists that whatever advantages the matrilinear system may have secured for women, only in a few cases can the system be in any way correlated with power or emancipation.

Theories of Subjection

In the primitive promiscuous group which anthropologists postulate in the pre-agricultural world,[15] women were of course in a sense the pivot of society, because paternity, whether as a social or a physiological fact, was as yet unrecognised. But as the family evolves, the central position of women is modified by countless new developments, and attempts to explain the facts now at our disposal as regards her subsequent social evolution have hitherto been singularly inconclusive. One high authority urges vaguely that the husband's power is greater amongst those peoples who reckon kinship through the father, than among those who reckon kinship through the mother only (Steinmetz). Another writer declares that the condition of women depends mainly on the abundance or lack of food (Hales).[16] A third contends that any early power women possessed was doomed through the rise of property and the connection of a property value with the women themselves (Mrs Hartley), and so on.

But is it not obvious that all these questions are subordinate to something far more fundamental which, perhaps precisely because it is so obvious, is perpetually overlooked by nearly every writer on the subject? Westermarck, for instance, attributes the subjection of women thoughout history to such general causes as the lack in women of the qualities of body and mind that are essential for personal independence, prevalent ideas and religious prejudices about the nature of women, the father's power over his daughter, whereby his authority is later transferred to the husband, and the narrowing influence of systems of society which may be contrasted with the complexity and wider interests of what we are pleased to term modern civilisation.[17] Such influences may no doubt have contributed their share, but it is strange that no mention should be made of the significance of war − of the influence which the reign of violence and the appeal to armed force as the deciding factor in every dispute, must have had on those whose virtue it is to possess 'qualities of body and mind' that are certainly ill adapted to secure 'personal independence' under such conditions.

The Neglected Factor

With a few exceptions it is probably true to say that woman has been subject to man in the past, and is still far from attaining complete emancipation, because in the past the fundamental fact in social life has been its open parade of physical violence. Wherever this background of physical violence has been temporarily obscured, there women have asserted their claim to equality with man. Whenever a country by natural advantages or social conditions has been able for a while to turn its thoughts to constructive efforts, and to the establishment of a system of justice, there, on the whole and in the long run, the cause of women's emancipation has advanced. In other cases her apparent freedom has been illusory or easily traced to some unusual transient circumstance. *Wars and rumours of wars have been her undoing in the past, and they remain the chief obstacle to her progress in the future.*

From this point of view let us examine the lesson of history. First of all let us consider once more the conditions of primitive life, and ask if it is not a little significant that Veblen,[18] the latest sociologist to review the whole body of evidence now at our disposal, finds himself forced to the view that in neolithic times (or throughout the whole age when woman occupied the position of honour to which we have referred above) mankind enjoyed a period of comparative peace and prosperity.[19] From the modern standard of emancipation the value of the benefits which women then enjoyed can, as we have shown, easily be exaggerated; but for the age in question such a degree of consideration on the part of men is hard to explain by any other hypothesis than that of Veblen. Only in virtue of comparative peace would primitive man have become an agriculturist, and have domesticated those animals and crop plants which date from neolithic times. Only in a peaceful age in which women were naturally associated with all that concerns fertility and growth could a religion have been evolved in which the deities were prevailingly female.

Mother-Right and Matriarchy

An instance of such tendencies developing in a direction more than usually favourable to the independence of women is to be found amongst the Khasis, on the borders of Assam. Sir Charles Lyall describes them as a vigorous and sturdy race. The mother is the head and source, and only bond of union of the family; she is the only real owner of property. The powers of sickness and death are all female, and the increase of the population is comparatively slow, this latter fact being probably due to 'the independence of the wife, and the facilities which exist for divorce.' They are a people cheerful in disposition, good tempered, and light-hearted by nature: fond of music: content to sit still and contemplate nature. 'The women are specially cheerful.' Finally, as one might expect, it is expressly recorded that the Khasis have enjoyed an unusual isolation from surrounding tribes, and are conspicuously 'devoid of anything approaching a martial spirit.'[20]

The real advantages of mother-right as such may not always have been great. In all probability they were greater according to the degree in which peaceful habits of life could be established, and the point to note is that such benefits as did affect women were possible only *where war and martial ideals were forced to take a secondary place in the life of the people.*

Given an agricultural community, and given the equipment of ideas with which primitive man works, an organisation of the family on the basis of mother-right is sufficiently natural; but, as we have seen, the mere existence of such a family system by no means ensures even the equality of women with men in the affairs of every day life. On the other hand the bene-ficial influence of peace and, vice versa, the detri-mental influence exercised by warfare as such on the position of women is remarkably well-supported by the actual facts. Thus it is instructive to find that Herbert Spencer,[21] after an independent investiga-tion of the evidence as regards the social condition of primitive societies, feels himself constrained to remark that while the status of women is habitually very low in tribes given to war and in modern mili-tarist nations, 'it is habitually very high in these primi-tive peaceful societies. The Bodo and the Dhimals, the Kocch, the Santals, the Lepchas, are monogamic, as were also the Pueblos; and along with their mono-gamy habitually goes a surperior sexual morality.' The behaviour to women is extremely good. The Santal treats the female members of his family with respect,[22] the Bodo and the Dhimals treat their wives and daughters with confidence and kindness.[23] Moreover, we are told concerning sundry of these unwarlike peoples that the status of children is also high; and there is none of that distinction of treat-ment between boys and girls which characterises mili-tarist societies.[24]

It is, in fact, amazing how the two factors of war and the position of women are invariably correlated in this manner in all accounts. Thus amongst the Eskimos warfare is practically unknown. Ross 'could not make the people of Baffin's Land understand the meaning of battles.'[25] Of the Western Eskimos we read, 'it not infrequently happens that the woman is the chief authority in the house,'[26] or elsewhere (Point Barrow) 'the women appear to stand on a footing of perfect equality with the men, both in the family and in the Community.'[27] With the Todas of India women 'hold a position in the family quite unlike what is ordinarily witnessed among Oriental nations' — says one writer. Why? 'The Todas,' we learn from another source, 'have the character of being most pacific.'

The Transition to Patriarchy

Exactly how peaceful was the primitive society in which mother-right originated and exactly how valuable the privileges it conferred may remain open questions, but there can certainly be no doubt as to the causes of the positive oppression of woman which have everywhere followed the rise of the patriarchal system. For this is essentially the product of a fighting age when men take active command of affairs. Population had multiplied and cattle increased sufficiently to give occasion or excuse for wanderings to and fro. A sufficient quantity of portable goods had been accumulated to tempt aggression when any tendency to collisions between groups was manifested. Society was reconstituted for aggression and defence rather than primarily for life, and above all (as regards historical development) the resulting capture of females by the victorious groups led to that institution of a permanent class of female slaves which has had so disastrous an influence for the degradation of women in every age and in every country where slavery has since prevailed. Mother-right can no longer flourish when warriors enter on the scene. But when Mrs Gasquoine Hartley remarks on the change that 'It was no more possible for society to be built up on mother-right alone than it is possible for it to remain permanently based on father-right,'[28] it is clear that she has omitted to consider the inevitable consequence of war, a neglect which vitiates her theory of the evolution of the women's movement in common with so many others. It is absolutely essential that we should realise that it is possible for society to remain permanently based on father-right, and that it *certainly will remain so based as long as and wherever wars and preparations for wars are an essential feature of civilisation.*

War and Slavery

The earliest and most usual source of slavery was war, just as subjection in later times is based on physical force. In China the slave class is composed primarily of prisoners of war. In ancient Egypt every early Pharaoh records the employment of prisoners of war as slaves. In Chaldaea there was a class of slaves largely consisting of captives from foreign races and their descendants, reinforced by native children sold by their fathers and women sold by their husbands.[29] Among the Hebrews the slave class consisted largely of captives taken in war (Deut. xx. 14.). Mohammedan slaves are chiefly captives and the same is true of ancient India, Greece and of Rome, where it was officially justified as a mitigation of the horrors of war.

The effect of slavery on women in ancient times can best be gathered by recalling what it meant in Christian America less than 100 years ago. The master could, whenever he liked, separate husband and wife; he could, if he pleased, commit adultery with the wife and was the absolute owner of all the children borne by her. The common rules of morality were not enforced on slaves, and even in Puritan New England female slaves in ministers' and magistrates' families bore children black and yellow without marriage; no one inquired who their fathers were, and nothing more was thought of it than the breeding of sheep or swine. And concerning the plantation slave quarters, Westermarck further records the universal testimony that 'the sexes were herded together promiscuously like beasts.' Under such circumstances — where morality and human life were valued so low — women could hope for little permanent improvement in their position. The double standard of morality which resulted, and the incentive which such a system has always given to tyranny and cruelty, have left an indelible mark wherever slavery has prevailed. Against its traditions women are still struggling, and it is important that the part here played by war should not be overlooked.

War and Polygamy

For largely due to the influence of war, and of its creation, slavery, is the practice of polygamy.[30] Men may be tortured, eaten, sacrificed or simply killed, but women and children are more usually carried off as slaves; not as ordinary slaves, but as household slaves, the slaves of the harem, with its almost universal characteristics, the conception of women as property, the extinction of the emotions of love as opposed to those of physical enjoyment, and the degradation thereby entailed. Warlike religions have always preserved these features, and the case of Mohammedanism is typical of the class.

In early times Arab women occupied a relatively high position, for Arab culture early reached a stage of civilisation associated, as Professor Robertson Smith[31] has told us, with ideas of peaceful opulence. In this period it is significant that women had rights and were respected; the veil and the harem system were unknown before Mohammed. But with the breakdown of their primitive culture an era of chronic inter-tribal warfare was inaugurated,[32] and by the time of Mohammed women had become mere chattels. 'A man can bear anything but the mention of his wives' is recorded as a representative male utterance of the period. There is a difference of opinion as to the actual change effected by Mohammedanism. Mohammed's own view of the part played by women is interesting, 'I have not left any calamity more hurtful to man than women'[33] and it is universally admitted that Mohammedanism (pre-eminently the religion of conquest) gives women a lower position than any other creed of modern times. Among the pirates who infested the Mediterranean, for instance, none were worse than the Moors. They are fanatical Mohammedans; cruel, revengeful and blood-thirsty. The chief amusement of adult Moors is the 'powder-play,' which consists of a type of military tournament. Slavery and slave auctions conducted like those of mules are a regular feature of their warlike life. The position of women is little better than a pampered slavery, and a striking indication of their general status may be found in the fact that young girls, much as amongst the warriors of Tahiti, are stuffed like chickens with paste-balls mixed with honey, or with spoonfuls of olive-oil and sesame, to give them the corpulence which sensuality requires.

Yet apart from their militarism there is nothing in the life of the Moors to lead to such degradation. Your typical Moor is a handsome fellow, characterised by marked dignity of demeanour, and distinctly intellectual. Whenever social conditions have given him a chance to free himself from perpetual savagery and bloodshed, he has shewn that bestiality and oppression of women is no more essential to his happiness than to that of other men. For nearly eight centuries, under her Mohammedan rulers, Spain set to all Europe a shining example of a civilised and enlightened state. Art, literature and science prospered as they prospered nowhere else in Europe. The surgeons and doctors of these Spanish Moors led the world in their art; women were encouraged to devote themselves to serious study, and a lady doctor was not unknown among the people of Cordova.[34] The Saracens in Spain had the merit of letting women share freely in their culture of all kinds.[35] They were in fact gradually losing their bellicose propensities and cultivating the gentler virtues, when their tendencies towards constitutionalism, and the refinement they had attained, gradually put them at the mercy of their Christian foes. They were forced not only to retain their military habits, but to call to their aid the fanatical Almovarides from Barbary — after which of course the social and intellectual life of Saracen Spain went the way of other civilisations which militarism without has successfully overwhelmed.[36]

The Religion of Conquest

In Turkey and in India the effect of militant Mohammedanism on women has been equally disastrous, but it will be more profitable to devote a few pages to the study of Militarism and Feminism in the East, and in Egypt, Greece, and Rome, before we proceed to discuss the similar features presented by the history of modern Europe. For the astonishing persistence with which the profound influence of militarism on the status and freedom of women has been ignored hitherto makes it desirable to collect the historical evidence over as wide a field as possible, and to make it accessible to all who are themselves in doubt, or who, being already convinced, may desire to convince others of the truth of their views.

Let us first consider the great civilisations of antiquity. Will anyone contest the verdict of that penetrating sociologist, Mr Havelock Ellis, that 'in their early stage, the stage of growth, as well as in their final stage, women tend to occupy a favourable position; while in their middle stage, *usually the stage of predominating military organisation on a patriarchal basis*, women occupy a less favourable position.'[37] But is it not equally clear that in the stage of growth the relatively favourable position of women is explained by the obvious fact that growth implies a people with something better to occupy its attention than quarrelling with its neighbours; while, in the final stage, though national organisation is based ultimately on the possibility of war, this potential pugnacity is generally obscured by complex institutions? So long as it is latent the emancipation of women, as we shall see, can never proceed very far.[38]

The Peaceful Egyptian

From this point of view it will at once be clear why in ancient Egypt women enjoyed a freedom and dignity higher than in other states of antiquity. 'It is the glory of Egyptian morality,' says Amélineau,[39] 'to have been the first to express the Dignity of Woman.' And the Egyptians, as Mrs Hartley has pointed out, 'were an agricultural and a conservative people. *They were also a pacific race. They would seem not to have believed in that illusion of younger races — the glory of warfare* ... Through the long centuries of civilisation they devoted their energies to the building up and preserving of their social organisation.' The italics are ours, and sufficiently emphasise our contention. Yet the same writer, like almost all others, does not press home her point, and entirely fails to grasp its significance for modern times. The high position of Egyptian women must clearly be connected with these peaceful propensities. 'From the beginning,' says Mr

Perris in his *History of War and Peace*,[40] 'the Egyptian appears the least martial of men,' with the result that the freedom of the women was a source of perpetual astonishment to the warlike Greeks from Herodotus to Diodorus. But the peaceful instincts of the people were overcome by their rulers, and it is significant that during the age of the martial Pharaohs Egypt was much like other militarist countries. It was only when the natural desire for peace could assert itself that women benefited. As Mr Gallichan has remarked, 'When the Egyptians became pacific, women enjoyed the social, civic and domestic advantages which were denied to them during the militant period.'[41]

As in the earlier instance of mother-right, it is not that the position of women in Egypt would necessarily give the modern champions of emancipation much ground for satisfaction; and, of course, there was no lack of warfare even in the land of the Pharaohs: but relatively to the age such honour as she allowed was a blessing of this comparative peace. This is all equally applicable to Babylon if we remember that the Babylonians were as a whole a less peaceful people than the Egyptians. In the earliest times women had equal rights with men; the code of Hamurabi shows these rights as circumscribed in the military age; while in Neo-Babylon, where war had receded into the background, equality again appears.[42]

Not less clear than the lesson of Egypt is the evidence of Greece and Rome. In the former, civilised woman reached her nadir as wife and mother. No other European civilisation has witnessed so complete a segregation of women for breeding purposes; while for companions the Athenians turned invariably to foreign courtesans throughout the whole military period. The Greek of history is, as we shall see, the most warlike of men, and his women suffer accordingly wherever military ideals prevail.

Sparta No Exception

It is somewhat surprising that Sparta is sometimes regarded as an exception to this suppression. People who so regard her must be exceedingly ignorant either of the state of affairs there prevailing, or of the meaning which women attach to the word freedom. In Sparta no one was free, as Dr Donaldson has so well shown in his *Woman in Ancient Greece and Rome*.[43] There was no regard for the individual. Men and women alike were subservient to one great military ideal. That was the price which woman had to pay in the only country in the world where she has been accorded an equal right with man to such physical and mental development as the nation could realise. How great was the sacrifice that Sparta made to militarism is shown by her failure to produce a single contribution to the thought of the world; but that her women were at least not more unhappily circumscribed than her men is so much to her credit. Such an ideal of a military stud farm is, happily, impossible of realisation in modern times, when celibates can no longer be placed under the ban of society, the age of marriage fixed, and all children who meet with the disapproval of the town council within whose jurisdiction they are born quietly put out of the way.[44]

Aristotle tells us that the superiority of the Greeks to the barbarians was shown, amongst other things, in the fact that the Greeks did not, like other nations, regard their wives as slaves — and slavery in ancient days was the symbol of warlike dominion. Happily, in Athens, the warrior's primal right was not rigidly enforced, but the degraded position of women on which Athenian culture was based is inexplicable, if the military organisation of the city state is left out of account. And it is important that we should realise this, for it is the Athenian social ideal which is still

93

held up in education before the eyes of the ruling classes of Europe!

Two Crystallised Traditions

(i) — The Hebrew Family

This brings us to a factor in the historical situation which we have already encountered in the case of mother-right — the tendency for traditions, and the customs and ideas in which traditions crystallise, to linger for centuries after the circumstances out of which they arose have passed away. The recognition of such survivals which impose themselves either through institutions or education on a people or a generation to which they do not properly belong is very necessary, if we are to understand the forces which assist in keeping women in their present position in modern times.

These forces include in all European countries for the last 1500 years first that quintessential relic of military morality, the Hebrew patriarchal ideal embedded in Christianity. The principle of crystallised traditions, for which we have to thank military necessities, is of course of very wide application. For instance, it will be objected to those who accuse militarism of having been the main cause of the degradation of women in every age, that priests no less than soldiers have conspired to effect her subjection. Thus our foremost living sociologist considers that 'religion has probably been the most persistent cause of the wife's subjection to her husband's rule.'[45] In reply to this we may quote the opinion of a famous modern militarist for what it is worth. He is answering the question: To what do we owe the establishment and maintenance of religious dogmas and a priestly caste? 'I suggest,' he says, 'that the origin of priestly power is really to be sought in the necessity of finding some means powerful enough to *compel tribes to combine for purposes of self-defence.* It was absolutely necessary to create a "hell" to have somewhere for the cowards to go to, and a "heaven" of course was the necessary antithesis.'[46] The italics are ours. But whether this generalisation can be substantiated or not, the influence of Hebrew ideas on Christianity is both marked and disastrous. The Hebrew idea of women is the idea of that primitive militarist, the patriarchal nomad. Professor J.A. Cramb[47] rightly remarks that 'If ever there were a race which seemed destined to found a world-empire by the sword it is the Hebrew. They make war with Roman relentlessness and with more than Roman ideality ... and march to music beside which all other war songs appear of no account − "Let my sword-hand forget, if I forget thee, O Jerusalem!" ' We may or may not approve of Lecky's remarks in his History of European Morals[48] on that 'common oriental depreciation of women' which the Jews shared; the fact remains that Judaism is in its original essence a militarist religion, the religion which conquered Canaan for its God of Battles.

'*Of the cities of these peoples which the Lord thy God giveth thee for an inheritance, thou shalt save nothing alive that breatheth.*' There are few records in history more revolting than the account in Numbers xxxi of the wrath of Moses with the children of Israel for saving the women of Midian alive, and the subsequent slaughter of married women; or that in 1 Chronicles xx of how David and Joab at Rabbah 'brought forth the people that were therein, and cut them with saws, with harrows of iron, and with axes,' and thus did they unto all the cities of the children of Ammon. On these two occasions women did not even have the advantage of the Divine command − 'The women and the little ones and the cattle shalt thou take for a prey unto thyself.' The warmest eulogy of a woman in the Old Testament is that bestowed on her who, with circumstances of the most aggravated treachery, had murdered the sleeping fugitive who had taken refuge under her roof.[49] It was the combined influence of these Jewish writings, and the conception (reinforced, we must remember, by the primitive mythology of Genesis) of women as the chief source of temptation to man which produced those fierce invectives against females in the early fathers, from whom official Christianity has since borrowed so much in the matter of moral precept.

(ii) — The Masculine Ideal

Secondly, there is the exclusively masculine ideal which runs through the whole of ancient literature, and which, as pointed out above, is impressed on the youth of both sexes today. They read (without realising the omission) of a man-made civilisation, of its wars, of its religion, of its love. It all seems quite natural; and hence the world today is not so *very* different, for are we not all alike thus inoculated for feminine ideals? The supreme beauty of the art of the warlike Greeks is, as Winckelmann first pointed out, 'rather male than female.'[50] The virtues of antiquity are the male virtues of courage, self-assertion, magnanimity, 'and above all,' as Lecky has reminded us, 'patriotism.'[51] Women were illustrious, not for their corresponding feminine virtues, but because they imitated their warrior males, as the Amazon, the Spartan mother, the Mother of the Gracchi[52] — women who fought, or who bore and sacrificed husbands and sons for battle. And the youth of modern Europe have not yet learned to reverence any other ideal.

These two influences have moulded the thought of

96

modern Europe almost to the exclusion of others, as far as national ethics are concerned. The result has been clearly pointed out by Principal Graham in his brilliant exposure of Militarism — *Evolution and Empire*.[53] 'It is the custom for those who have imbibed their ideas of war between nations at school from the Classics and from the Old Testament, and who have not thought it necessary to revise their conceptions . . . to consider that some foreign nation may be our foe, as an individual may have an individual enemy.' From these two sources come their conception of war as natural and inevitable; and hence, too, significantly enough, they derive their ideas of the proper sphere of woman. And bearing in mind these facts let us briefly summarise the story of the epoch whence the influences in question arise.

A Panorama of War

First of all as to the military foundations of social life in those ancient Empires whose ideals are still so largely our own. 'Ancient civilisations appear to us as an immense battlefield, a vast cemetery of peoples,' says the Italian historian Ferrero.[54] Tribes, nations, great empires and small states only emerge in order to destroy the tribes, peoples, empires and states that preceded them, to be in their turn destroyed by other rivals. Nations seemed only born to die a violent death; their lives generally began with a victory and ended with a defeat, which entailed, in most cases, not merely the effacing from history of the name of a state, but the physical destruction of an entire society. Every work of art, of science, of politics appears to have had no other object in the distant past than that of fostering war, of covering the earth with costly ashes. A few exceptions there may be. Egypt was one, but as regards Greece and Rome the above description holds good. Think of the case of Athens who by her pride and cupidity provoked a conflict with Sparta, in which she obstinately persevered, always attempting new military undertakings, till after the Sicilian campaign she found herself ruined and undone.[55]

But in Athens, as in the centres of many other powerful Empires, warlike preoccupations were slowly beginning to exert a diminishing influence on the weary populace, and social affairs (including the women's movement, of which we hear so much in Aristophanes), to gain more serious consideration, when all hopes of peaceful development were suddenly shattered by the bellicose activities of Macedonia. From the earliest dawn of their history the Greeks, except for this one brief moment, and in certain isolated areas, never gave woman a chance. War followed war in unending succession. In fact, as Professor William James has remarked, 'Greek history is a panorama of war for war's sake ... of the utter ruin of a civilisation which in intellectual respects was perhaps the highest the earth has ever seen.'[56] In Rome the 'Pax Romana' allowed signs even more hopeful for women to make their appearance; but in Rome, as in Greece, women were once more baulked by wars. War had followed war for century after century, and now, finally, the Hebrew marriage system, embedded, as a survival from the age of militaristic patriarchs, in the practical ethics of Christianity[57] combined with the renewed inroads of warriors from the East, who ranged over Europe for the dark centuries which followed, to blast the hopes of peace and of women until yesterday.

Can anyone doubt that the prevalence of war has been fundamentally responsible for the subjection of women in every age? Ideas, prejudices — but these are for the most part crystallisations of earlier warlike traditions, reinforced by the promptings of fear — fear that the fighting strength of the nation might be diminished if softer pleadings were heard. So hopeless, so foolish, did the thought of emancipation seem that hardly a voice was raised against the customs that prevailed. Violence between nations or within a nation settled all collective disputes, and each individual relied ultimately on his physical force to solve his own problems with his equals, or to keep his inferiors in their proper place. In such a world woman simply sinks and remains submerged. In such a world there was no hope for a movement of emancipation. It is needless to seek for other causes.

Chapter III

The Lesson of History — II

*'Authentic tidings of invisible things . . .
And central peace subsisting at the heart
Of endless agitation.'* — Wordsworth[58]

Between the final stage of Roman civilisation and the
rise of anything approaching the degree of freedom
which women had there attained, it is necessary to
leap over considerably more than 1,000 years of warfare so perpetual that the idea of emancipation
scarcely arises.[59] But in modern times the influence
of militarism, wherever found, has been precisely the
same as in ancient days. From the mass of evidence
available from every country let us take one example,
whose lesson is so obvious, and whose effects so far-
reaching, that it admirably typifies the rest. It also has
the advantage of allowing us not to get too near
home, and so relieves us from the necessity of discussing the views of Lord Curzon or Wilhelm II[60] as to
the true function of women in the social order!

Napoleon and his Legacy

Nowhere is the influence of militarist ideas on women
seen more clearly than in the work of Napoleon,
which even to this day remains at the foundation of so

much that is evil in Europe. 'Glory abroad, efficiency at home' was Napoleon's motto, and everything was made subservient to the requirements of a military policy. The whole social organisation of the Consulate is based on such a policy, for in all his state-craft Napoleon, as a recent authority has strongly insisted, 'was following his own inclinations as a military commander, used to rigid discipline.'[61] Hence he was led to undo much of the legislation of the Revolution. The ideal of the revolutionists was individual liberty. 'They had sought to make of the family a little Republic, founded on the principles of liberty and equality, but in the new code the paternal authority reappeared . . . The family was thenceforth modelled on the idea dominant in the State, *that authority and responsible action pertained to a single individual*.'[62] The father controlled everything, and the customs thus established by Napoleon in the interests of a military organisation have, as Dr Rose points out, 'had a mighty influence in fashioning the character of the French, as of the other Latin peoples, *to a ductility that yields a ready obedience to local officials, drill-sergeants, and the central government*.' Again the italics are ours, and show the ideals which animated Napoleon in his determination of the part women were to play in the social life of France. In every respect he used his mighty influence deliberately to depress her legal status, and he prescribed a formula of obedience to be repeated by the bride to her husband. In this respect the views of Napoleon were, as Ostrogorski emphatically puts it,[63] 'those of an Oriental despot. In his capacity of a man of war, he added to the duties of women that of furnishing soldiers to the army.' 'A husband,' said Napoleon, 'ought to have an absolute control over the actions of his wife. He has a right to say to her, "Madam, you shall not go out," or "Madam, you belong to me body and soul." ' Even the drawing up of the article providing that the 'wife owes obedience to her husband' did not appear to Napoleon sufficiently striking. The presiding official must be clothed in imposing garb, and speak in solemn actions to invest the maxim with an awful and unforgettable authority. The laws of divorce which had been gradually relaxed in favour of women were re-established in the strictest form; while in matters of social morality the disastrous enactments of the Code Napoleon are too well known to need enumeration here.[64] Such was the spirit of the system whereby France was remodelled, and Professor Esmein[65] records that in addition to France Belgium has preserved it; the Rhine provinces only ceased to be subject to it on the promulgation of the civil code of the German Empire. Numerous more recent codes have taken it as a model – Dutch, Italian, Portuguese, Spanish, Central and South American. And thus its influence remains, a monument of military masculinity, and a menace to feminism wherever it has appeared.

La Gloire

In France itself the tradition of Napoleon was dominant throughout the whole of the last century. And the military ideals thus impressed on the whole nation can alone explain the insignificant part played in the social system of French public life by women who are in certain respects the most advanced in Europe. 'The study of French militarism serves to acquaint us with the life and structure of this social system,' as Ferrero has pointed out in his brilliant essay on Militarism and Caesarism in France;[66] and, writing of the state of affairs prevailing in the nineties, he goes on to show that essentially military ideas are still most popular in France, more especially with the cultured classes.

Although war between civilised nations is coming to be considered by many as only tolerable when urged in defence of some principle, 'the general sentiment amongst educated Frenchmen is favourable to war, and little tempered by moral considerations.' They deem it a great thing, *per se*, for a nation to conquer; political and military supremacy are regarded as the first factors in the superiority of a civilisation. Hence a conquered nation that has not yet taken revenge must necessarily consider its civilisation in decadence. The policy which aims at the annexation of fresh territories in Europe, Asia, or Africa, is considered excellent in itself, as by increasing the area of an empire its glory and power is also increased, wherefore the cost in men and money is held of small account.

Thus, concludes Ferrero, the cultured classes, if not the whole nation, accept in silence ideals which correspond so ill to the requirements of the age. 'Military traditions are transmitted from generation to generation, and fossilised into integral parts of the administration.' The majority does not and cannot rule in France; the various coteries and small minorities, who from time to time come into power, take no trouble to reform the Government. 'The only aim of a ministry is to satisfy the clients which raised it to power. All the rest, the reform of abuses and so forth, except what is brought about by the force of circumstances, is treated by the various Governments with a very Mussulman indifference.' The word Mussulman is strikingly appropriate here, for the subjection of women is essentially one of those abuses which the religion of conquest has persistently regarded with supreme indifference.

But in the last two decades a great change had come over France, and militarism was already on the decline. More and more attention was being directed towards social abuses, and a feminist movement was yearly gaining in strength. In the twentieth century it is rather Germany that has openly sacrificed social welfare to the consolidation of military power, with results even more disastrous to feminism than those we have already recorded.

A Naval Incident

Finally, as regards Great Britain herself. Throughout the centuries it has been the same story. The position of women has risen or fallen according as war or peace was in the ascendant, not contemporaneously, perhaps, but the connection can always be traced. In general, England has been spared the continuous and demoralising warfare of her continental neighbours, and on the whole the position of women has been higher in England than on the continent. But that it could never be very high is clear from even a few instances. Let us recall for instance that in 1379 'Sir John Arundel's squadron was overtaken by a storm and *sixty women who were on board were thrown into the waves* to lighten the vessels. Some of these women had willingly accompanied the fleet; *others had been forcibly carried to sea.*'[67] Consider the social conditions here implied – especially by the final words italicised. Of what value is it to quote the names of high-born ladies who attained a certain influence and power in centuries when military domination could be manifested in actions like this? Of what value is it to refer to the system of 'chivalry' which men often speak of as something to which women should look back with pride and gratitude, if the greatest power of Europe had learnt no better manners than these at its close? It is thus that we must explain the late appearance of women's demand for equality – that *it seemed to her mere folly to dream of it in the midst of the violence generated by ceaseless wars*. It is thus that we must explain the denial of education to women in all ages — that *it seemed folly to give education to anyone who could not bear arms*. Exceptions there were — abbesses, royal ladies, even queens; but what use were these to women as a whole? Are there not queens today?

Spencer's Forgotten Discovery

Has anyone really made us understand the true reasons why the political emancipation of women, after a full fifty years of agitation and propaganda since its first intrusion into practical politics in 1865,[68] is still unrealised? The movement, as will be generally agreed, first raised its head when a period of profound peace had allowed a recovery from the exhaustion of the Napoleonic Wars, and the development of industrialism to an extent which had temporarily obscured the militaristic basis of social organisation. What prevented the speedy realisation of women's ideals? Many reasons have been advanced, and in most of them there is no doubt a substratum of truth. But is there not a special significance in the discovery of Herbert Spencer, whose practised eye detected another growing movement and the simultaneous progress of other ideals? Side by side with the movement for emancipation he saw the rise of military spirit which counteracted it, and which today threatens to strangle its rival as on so many occasions in the past. In 1876 Spencer noted in the first volume of his *Sociology* that militarism was reviving in Britain. In 1882 he returned to the subject (in Vol. III, p. 590) with a reference to 'the revival of military activity which has of late been so marked that our illustrated papers are, week after week, occupied with little else than scenes of warfare. Within the military organisation itself we may note the increasing assimilation of the volunteer forces to the regular army, now going to the extent of proposing to make them available abroad, so that instead of defensive action, for which they were created, they can be used for offensive action,' and so forth; a most instructive analysis and worthy of serious study.

Were Spencer alive today he would have been surprised even at his own foresight, though he did not go on to show the connection between militarism and the failure of the women's movement with which we are here concerned. Is it not only too evident that the chief retarding factor has been perpetually neglected by advocates of women's rights? We have been deceived by the veneer of industrialism that had obscured the real danger. We had forgotten that pregnant passage in which Spencer elsewhere casually grants the main position we are here concerned to establish. He is dealing with peaceful peoples, and contrasting them with warrior races. In the peaceful tribes, he remarks, there is a marked superiority both in social and domestic relations. He instances, as we have already instanced, the superior position of women amongst such peoples as are not addicted to war; and he turns to investigate the facts in more modern times. What is the effect of industrialism on the position of the individual? The answer is complicated by the fact that 'we encounter the difficulty that the personal traits proper to industrialism, are like the social traits, mingled with those proper to militancy. It is manifestly thus with ourselves. A nation which, besides its occasional serious wars, is continually carrying on small wars with uncivilised tribes; a nation which is mainly ruled in Parliament and through the press by men whose school discipline led them during six days in the week to take Achilles for their hero, and the seventh to admire Christ; a nation which, at its public dinners, habitually toasts its army and navy before toasting its legislative bodies;

cannot allow the characteristics proper to industrialism to be shown with clearness. In independence, in honesty, in truthfulness, in humanity, its citizens are not likely to be the equals of the uncultured but peaceful peoples above described. All we may anticipate is an approach to those moral qualities appropriate to a state undisturbed by international hostilities; and this we find.'

This we find! This we shall always find. And one of the things we always thus find — and some day perhaps the women's movement will be reunited by the realisation of the discovery — is that these international hostilities are much the most dangerous enemy of emancipation with which women have to struggle. One day perhaps a woman who does not actively work for peace will become as anomalous as the Christian who is content to take his ethical guidance chiefly from the Mosaic dispensation. But the New Gospel has not yet found its apostles. We are still waiting for the leaders.

Signs of Progress

In the meantime we may learn not a little from the progress that has already been made. Two great steps have been taken. Violence between individuals has ceased; men no longer carry swords; and it is possible for women to walk abroad in towns (though not everywhere in the country), provided it is broad daylight, without an armed escort! That has made it possible for her to raise her voice in public, and to appear freely in public places, whereas while swords were necessary it was not possible. And secondly, violence as between masters and their slaves has ceased. Thereby a great incentive to the degradation of woman has been removed.

Militarism itself, as it seemed to some, had vanished

except as a survival; and the woman's movement arose as the world slumbered in apparent security. But militarism was there all the while, as women are realising to their cost. Will they realise fully and in time? On which side will the united efforts of the most hopeful movement the world has yet seen be thrown? The war can have many results, but nothing is inevitable. *Nothing save the downfall of woman's hopes if militarism should finally emerge triumphant.*

Chapter IV

'When nations were devoted to continual warfare the duties of men were defined, and, while the women were left behind to care for the children and perform the baser services, the men went forth to war, or took upon them the affairs of the State. This distinction has been preserved. No moral or intellectual progress has been sufficient to shake it. All pretensions to equality have been contradicted by the treatment of women, by their exclusion from the most honourable forms of labour, and by withholding from them social, civil, and political rights.' — Professor Lester F. Ward[69]

In some respects it must be regarded as an unfortunate feature of the modern women's movement that its origins date from a period when, almost more than at any time either before or since, the true significance of militarism was obscured by economic and scientific developments and by the insular character of the land where it first gained a propagandist force.

Mill's Important Omission

Since the publication of Mill's *Subjection of Women*[70] the whole course of female emancipation may be traced in an unbroken line down to the present day. Mill summed up the opinions of feminists in the middle of the nineteenth century in language so clear that even today, to the latest historian of the movement, 'its popularity is likely to increase rather than to diminish.'[71] Hence it is of considerable importance to appreciate the atmosphere in which it was written in order that we may not be led into a position of false security by the important omission which can be detected at certain points in Mill's analysis. Nowhere is this omission more clearly seen than in his statement that 'the social subordination of women stands out an isolated fact in modern social institutions; a single relic of an old world of thought and practice, as if a vast temple of Jupiter Olympius occupied the site of St Paul's and received daily worship.'

Had Mill written today he would certainly have revised this judgement, just as the woman's movement will be forced to revise its official statements of the conditions of progress in the future, by the recognition of that other legacy from ages when the fittest found it so difficult to survive — militarism and international pugnacity. The connection between warfare and male domination in the past would be granted by many who imagine that this connection nevertheless ceased at some moment when modern history is supposed to begin. But unfortunately their nebulosity cannot be justified. Militarism and an androcentric culture go hand in hand; and together they oppose that ideal of social co-operation on which the women's movement must ever base itself. And that this is so is not only the lesson of history, but is clear from general considerations.

The Brutalising Effects of War

Our standard authorities whose works still mould the thought of the rising generation have been far too ready to use phrases implying that war and its accompaniments were a thing of the past. But none of those few who have troubled to study the social effect of warlike habits is more instructive than Bagehot,[72] who goes so far as to ask tentatively whether 'the spirit of war does not still colour our morality far too much.' But so intent is he on the softer growths that 'have now half-hidden the old and harsh civilisation *which war made*' that he allows himself to imply, as these last words do imply, that war no longer determines the essentials of social structure. Events are proving him wrong; but just because war is now revealed as a more fundamental factor in modern life than Bagehot supposed, his estimate of the effects of militarist organisation is all the more valuable as an impartial analysis.

All that may be called 'grace' as well as virtue, he tells us,[73] is not nourished by war and preparations for war; humanity, charity, a nice sense of the rights of others, it certainly does not foster; insensibility to human suffering is an essential part of the legacy of war to the world. The trained warrior does not readily revolt from the things of war, and one of the principal of these is human pain. Men have become more tender to one another not because they have improved but because there are fewer soldiers: for soldiers as such, soldiers educated simply by their trade, such thoughts and feelings are too hard to understand. But the essential point is reached when we are told of the 'contempt for physical weakness and for women which marks early society. The non-combatant population is sure to fare ill during the ages of combat.' Belgium, Poland, Galicia, Scarborough, to say nothing of Cardiff[74] — it is a pity that Bagehot is not alive to bring his analysis up to date!

But it is not only by its insensibility to that human suffering and cruelty against which women for ever revolt, and by its contempt for physical weakness, that war stands in the way. Such an atmosphere is fatal to the reform of social abuses. But militarism goes further and creates the institutions whereby such an evil is crystallised. It creates by its own natural requirements that nucleus of exclusively male professions and of exclusively male direction which is the most formidable barrier opposed to women today. It is formidable because of its long tradition, for it is rooted in the necessities which primitive warfare created. The characteristic institution whereby the primitive warrior secured control of affairs and set the tone of society was the Man's House. 'Over the greater part of the world,' we have been told by an anthropologist,[75]

'from the South Pacific Islands, through Australia, Melanesia, Polynesia, Africa and America, an institution has been observed common to nearly all savage tribes called the "Man's House." The savage, instead of living a simple domestic life with wife and child, lives a double life. He has a domestic home and a social home. In the domestic home are his wife and family; in the Man's House is passed all his social civilised life.

'To the Man's House he goes when he attains maturity. It is his public school, his university, his club, his public-house. Even after marriage, it is in the Man's House he mainly lives. For a woman to enter the Man's House is usually tabu; the penalty is often death.'

But what is most significant from our point of view is its military aspect:

'The entertainment of strangers, all contact with news from the outside world, is reserved for the Man's House.

There he discusses the affairs of the tribe, there holds his parliament; in a word, a Man's House is "the House" and has all its "inviolable sanctity." '

The Man's House still exists, but it has added new buildings to its once simple structure. In it a nation's affairs are still discussed, and it also succeeds in finding room for Law, Medicine, Education, Church. And why this persistence and this extension? Because that body which had supreme control of the affairs of war in the tribe, and whose business it was to provide money for war in the nation which succeeded to the tribe, has slowly and consistently extended its sphere of influence to all departments of human life. The state is still constituted primarily as if for war. When the noise of battles cannot for the moment be heard, this military foundation is obscured by a myriad mushroom social growths, and even women dare to raise their heads and demand that voice in affairs which taxation or oppression seems to necessitate. But at the sound of the martial trump the graves are once more opened, and the reforms and aspirations of peace laid peaceably to rest.

The androcentric bias which military organisation creates is seen in the development of those exclusively male professions into which women are still trying to force an entry. The direction or control of all these by men alone has gained and still gains colour and sanction from the exclusively male control, which, in its own sphere, war demands. And not war alone, but that fear of war which directs much of our social life in times of peace. But the Man's House has not only multiplied its functions; it has extended its activities in a new and unexpected direction. Though still dominated by considerations of military expediency – army and navy estimates, foreign policy, and the flag which trade shall follow – it is forced more and more to interfere with the affairs of the family and in particular with the life and work of woman. To the authority of man inside the home is added the external authority of the Man's House as such — that house which women may not enter, since war and preparation for war which still determine its action in so many ways are the concern of man alone.

The Perversion of Industry

From these direct and inevitable characteristics of a state organised for war, let us turn to the perversion by militarism of the forces which might be expected to work for peace. In modern times the hope of women has lain in the industrial developments of the past two centuries. Industrial development which like the movement for emancipation not only demands peace in its own interests but is itself directly conducive to a pacific mode of life. Industry has been woman's special sphere whether in its origins[76] or in the later ages when she made in the house itself[77] the soap, candles, beer, bread, sheets, blankets, boots, clothes, with which she has since migrated to the factory. The independent wage which she there earned encouraged her to think of an independent life; the discarding of weapons of aggression and defence in civil life and the victory of internal order over personal violence enables her to live alone. Industrialism flourished on peace — and industrialism it was which gave birth to the idea of emancipation. Industrialism of itself encourages the forces which make for peace — the smooth working of the industrial machine abhors the inroads of violence; the exchange of goods implies a mutual understanding, production and salesmanship, an appreciation of the interest and desires of others which work directly against the military conceptions of forcible appropriation and the hostility of groups; in a word those patient and peaceful habits of industrious construction give a value to the work of man's hands which is entirely alien to the habits of the warriors who ply their trade of destruction as we know it in history. It has been well said that in marketing[78] woman is in her element, but the 'marketing' of war is to requisition, to commandeer, to billet.

Industry and commerce thus taken in and for themselves tend in the direction of peace, but this peaceful tendency is only too often overshadowed so long as the traditions of militarism prevail. 'England indeed grew ever more warlike as she grew more commercial,' says Sir John Seeley. 'Commerce in itself may favour peace, but when commerce is artificially shut out by a decree of government from some promising territory, then commerce just as naturally favours war.'[79] Thus we cannot look for any permanent improvement from the operation of economic forces alone. As long as public opinion is not convinced on other grounds of the sacrilegious folly of war, so long will the opportunity of war engender war itself: for men trained in the ethics of imperialism will apply that ethic to the advancement of their individual interests in the business world. We do not need to attribute the whole of the spirit of capitalistic competition to the influence of military ideals in order to acknowledge the great part which the latter have played in directing the industrial development in the past two centuries. Is not Admiral Mahan[80] the evangelist of all Sea Powers of both the New World and the Old? Are his works not held up to the admiration of every public school boy in England today — and have they not profoundly influenced the military preparation not only of England and America but in an even more striking manner of Germany and Japan? And what is his gospel? 'Governments,' he emphatically declares, 'are corporations, and corporations have no souls ... they must put first the rival interests of their own people. Predominance forces a nation to seek markets, and where possible to control them to its own advantage by preponderating force, the ultimate expression of which is possession ... an inevitable link in a chain of logical sequences: industry, markets, control, navy bases.' Precisely, and already in his teens the businessman unconsciously applies the lesson. Business firms are corporations ... no souls ... ultimate expression ... inevitable link ... logical sequences: and we wonder why the harsh ideals of barbarism survive in the modern world where national militarism has been reinforced by that industrial militarism which deserves no better name. Is it not here significant that the only point at which women have hitherto seriously impinged on the scene of strife is in the 'Women's Co-operative Guild'?[81] Perhaps Miss Llewellyn Davies will one day be known as the Florence Nightingale of Industrial Warfare.

The Perversion of Religion

But marked as is the domination of the industrial world by military ideals, industry is not more unfortunate than other tendencies which make for peace and favour emancipation. In spite of all that Christianity has done to soften the heart of the world it is doubtful whether any body of ethical teaching has so often been adapted to meet the requirements of militarists as that contained in the Gospels. 'The Lord Jesus Christ is not only the Prince of Peace, He is the Prince of War too,' wrote Charles Kingsley in order to justify the Crimean War;[82] 'He is the Lord of Hosts, the God of armies, and whoever fights in a just war has Christ for his Captain and his Leader.' And since no people as a whole ever yet fought in a war which they did not conceive to be just, the Sermon on the Mount does not in itself allow us to hope that official Christianity will refrain from subjecting its behests to modern interpretation. And apart from this general disadvantage we must remember that militarism is quite capable of using the purest religious motives deliberately for its own purposes. 'The soldier knows no law but force,' said Napoleon, 'sees nothing but force and measures everything by force. The civilian only looks to the general welfare. The characteristic of the soldier is to wish to do everything despotically.' What was Napoleon's religion? A Christian may well hesitate to answer this question, but there is no doubt as to the way in which the Patron Saint of all who 'do everything despotically' conceived of religion in the interests of the military ideal. In 1807 Napoleon thus formulated his ideals on a sound useful education for girls. 'We must begin with religion in all its severity. Do not admit any modification of this. We must train up believers, not reasoners. The weakness of women's brains, the unsteadiness of their ideas, *their function in the social order* . . . all can only be attained by religion.' They were to learn a little geography and history but no foreign language; above all to do plenty of needle-work.[83] From the Code Napoleon (cf. p. 102) we know what is meant by 'their function in the social order'. But it is only from his biographers that we can learn the part which religion may be made to play in a militarist world: and the actual effect of Napoleon's ideas on the movement for the emancipation of women will be clear to anyone who remembers the prominent share taken by women during the revolution, and compares it with the scanty activities (cf. p. 102 above) of women in the social life of France during the century which followed.

Similar instances could be given from every country, and one of the most instructive is to be found in the writings of Colonel F. N. Maude, C.B., England's leading military writer, whose standpoint is well indicated by the quotation which we reproduce on page 133. In his *War and the World's Life* he frankly faces the problem how to win the Churches to his point of view. He remarks (p. x.) 'It is not easy to suggest how the clergy are to be approached in such a matter — it is too largely a question of the individual employed' on such propaganda! He adds, 'But much has been done in the past few years.'

The instance of Napoleon has already introduced us to the perversions which education may similarly suffer; and here the effect of militarism is even more marked.

The Perversion of Education

From earliest childhood the modern infant is nurtured in an atmosphere of war. Its very cradle is loaded with popguns, leaden soldiers, drums, and trumpets, the forerunners of the forts which it storms when it can scarcely walk, and of the rifle and sword bigger than itself which glorify the nursery on the first available Christmas Day. As soon as it can be trusted to appreciate differences of clothing, the uniform of Dragoon and Hussar make their appearance, or a cocked hat, which does duty as a symbol of Nelson or Napoleon. Then come the histories where the military exploits of an Alexander, a Caesar, a Turenne, or a Marlborough gradually dwarf in the infant mind even the ever-present warriors of the Old Testament — the heroes for whom the God of Battles made the sun stand still, while, like others in later times, the edge of their sword imposed a higher civilisation on the hapless tribes of Canaan! History proper begins when lists of warriors and dates of battles can first conveniently be memorised. About 90 per cent of the population escape with a few such lists, and leave school at thirteen or fourteen with a vague memory of a few outstanding national warriors and of martial exploits chronologically arranged. A few go further and perfect this knowledge, and of these again a small proportion pass on to those abodes of learning — the universities. What knowledge is assumed in the average student of history when he enters the university? Let the late Regius Professor of History at Cambridge reply. For years his duty was to inspire the best of them, and there is little evidence that matters have improved since his day. This is how he used to open his lectures to these youths already entered on manhood:

Hitherto perhaps you have learned names and dates, lists of kings, lists of battles and wars! The time now comes when you are to ask yourselves, to what end? For what practical purpose are these facts collected and committed to memory?[84]

At the age of nineteen then it is at length permissible to ask, Why have I learnt this list of battles? But when we remember how infinitesimal a proportion of the community are privileged to continue their studies to this advanced age, it is clear that in the country as a whole the story of national wars and their makers forms practically the whole historical equipment of the voter. The slight improvement which was at length becoming discernible had, however, made but little headway. The average voter, the average municipal councillor, even — we may surely add — the average member of parliament, still thinks of the past in terms of warriors and battles; and since it is largely from his ideas of the past that he judges the present, it is small wonder that the male ideal prevails. And as in Parliament, so in the school. The men who write the histories are obsessed with this point of view, and so long as national rivalries loom so large there is little hope of change. All reformers, men and women alike, will have constantly to struggle with the traditions imposed on them in early years: and for women the case is aggravated by the fact that men for the most part still monopolise the writing of history which women must read, and men still direct the examinations by which the course of reading is so largely determined. It is small wonder therefore to find Mrs Charlotte Wilson[85] complaining of the utter inadequacy of existing histories as far as an understanding of the position of women is concerned. She explains, though without any reference to the influence of war, that as the individual man gradually emerged as a responsible, economically independent citizen from tribal and mediaeval corporate life, with its concomitants of slavery and of serfdom, the woman remained the adjunct of the man. 'She was his belonging; a creature attached civically and economically to him and under his control, and industrial history does not deal with her except incidentally. Her work, and its relation to her means of subsistence, *are taken for granted and practically ignored by our historians.* Consequently at every stage in our national economic development research into original contemporary sources must be made to discover facts about women as workers and consumers. With all deference to Rogers, Ashley, Toynbee, Hasbach and Cunningham, the economic history of this country from the point of view of the workers, to say nothing of the women workers, has yet to be written.'

The italics are ours, and they reveal what one might have expected from the foregoing discussion. The influence of militarism on education is a grievous legacy, with far-reaching consequences. And its workings are all the more insidious because when all have been impregnated alike it is particularly hard to inaugurate a change.

The whole organisation of our educational system is influenced by the obsessions of military administration. Children in the elementary school are for the most part still literally drilled in the various subjects scheduled by the Educational Headquarters Staff. 'Blind, passive, unintelligent obedience is the basis on which the whole system of Western education has been reared,' says Mr Edmond Holmes.[86] Why? Not entirely owing to the Doctrine of Original Sin, as Mr Holmes would have us believe. There have been other reasons. Take the case of that glorious warrior, Frederick the Great — to come no nearer to modern times! He was under no illusions as to Original Sin. But he knew the value of obedient soldiers: as a great educationalist has pointed out, 'He used the elementary school to make the masses stupid and to *drill obedient subjects*.' Almost all that was taught in the schools was the repetition of tags from the Bible, of hymns and of the catechism, though Frederick himself declared that 'religion was made to deceive men.'[87] Such instances can be multiplied all over the world.

Thoughts on Sports

And in the higher schools the cloven hoof is seen even more clearly. The Battle of Waterloo may or may not have been won on the playing fields of Eton, but if not, it was hardly the fault of Etonian organisation. Society itself begins by breaking children in to a game of killing before their minds act independently. It smears the blood of the dead fox or mutilated otter on the cheek of the little boy or girl who is in at the death for the first time. It goes on at Eton, half a century after Arnold abolished it at Rugby,[88] to

121

accustom him to the callous fun of the hare-hunt. He maims more than he kills, and the creatures which give him the best sport are precisely those that die hardest, after the longest struggle with terror and exhaustion. The English public schools are designed to turn out an imperial race, a race of warriors, and it is not without significance that they are constructed on the barracks system, and that their sport is all mimic warfare. Organised games, of which for many reasons England is justly proud, were the product of the fifties, and this is how those who supported their introduction defended them — 'In these hard contested matches will be found by no means the worst competitive examinations for those of our gallant youth who, from a more favoured development of body than of brain, will and must take to the profession of arms. Many a fine fellow who would fail lamentably in extracting a cube-root will, in after life, face an enemy's square, and break it effectually.'[89] We may compare with this a passage in one of the latest and most popular public school novels[90] which by the best authorities is acknowledged to give a true picture of the atmosphere of such schools today, where the hero's bosom friend remarks: 'The Head says a fellow who plays the brute at school, often turns out a ripping good chap afterwards. If he gets into the Army I daresay he'd make a first-rate officer.' We are left in doubt as to whether this is intended as a compliment to the army or is merely an attempt to justify bullying. That there may however be some connection between the two is seen in the observation of a writer in the *Daily News* during the correspondence which followed the publication of the book, that 'bullying in my opinion forms an essential and valuable feature of the public school system.'

The Two Spirits

In any case the success of sport has also been its nemesis, and shortly before the war broke out the Headmaster of Dulwich[91] was actually urging that 'the best thing is to find some substitute for an overpowering desire to excel in games, and some rival for them in a young man's esteem' — and his remedy is compulsory military service in schools and colleges! A similar demand has been made by the late Lecturer in Military History at Manchester, that soldiers should be appointed elementary schoolmasters in order that 'from the very first the children may be taught to look up to and respect the wearers of the King's uniform' and that in the schools 'the youth of both sexes should learn what the Empire really means and is.' The learned writer is appalled by the problem of 'how to bring home to the millions of the working classes, from whom ultimately our fighting men are derived, the idea that their country, as they see it, is a conception worth dying for.' To be willing to die in this manner they need to be fairly sensible, 'sensible enough to answer to the verbal appeal of some straightforward soldierly chaplain' — therefore in addition to a sound religion a sound education is of course essential. We may well look forward with anxiety to the spirit which is to dominate the schools of the future. For there are two spirits abroad. One we have allowed to speak for itself: the other may be compressed into a few words and they are the words of a woman — the greatest of modern teachers — 'How many times social problems centre about the necessity of rousing man from a state of "obedience" which has led him to be exploited and brutalised.'[92]

Such then are the characteristics of militarism in all ages, and such the false standards it has set up and is still preserving. In every country in the world it still proves itself, whether it threatens within or without, the greatest foe of progress.

In England, as we have seen (p. 105), the reality of its power was obscured, and it is impossible to lay too much emphasis on the influences which have enabled the British Isles to enjoy a century of peace at home and yet to retain the warrior spirit untarnished. For as a nation Britain has been perpetually at war. We have the surprising fact that though during the Chartist riots[93] 'it became absolutely unsafe for an officer in uniform to be seen alone in the streets,' so that uniform was even discarded for a time for safety's sake, the nation has never for a moment entirely lost that underlying militarism which ever and anon has demonstrated its potent effect on social organisation. The reason is to be found in the picturesque phrase of the military historian who so often throws light on dark places. 'India and the colonies *still kept alive the sacred flame.* India particularly proved our *true salvation.*'[94] India in fact could always be relied upon to provide first-rate fighting practice! To India has gone the flower of the nation's manhood and of its administrative ability: and trained in the same school were the men who have in reality controlled the social destinies of the nation. Apart from such distant warfare we must also remember that the warrior spirit of England has been able to spend itself fruitfully and unobtrusively on the high seas, and to defend the island nucleus from war's alarms. So at home there was peace in actuality; and, as we have seen, Mill himself wrote in the midst of peace. But, contemporaneous with the rise of the woman's movement, there rose the new imperialism. The Crimea and the Mutiny had aroused the public mind: there followed the Volunteer movement,[95] Sir John Seeley, Admiral Mahan, the Navy League, national expansion and an international jealousy in which all countries emulously participated until the great Day of Reckoning arrived — 1914, and the women of England still without even their votes.

An Instructive Chorus

But England was able to make a start, in virtue of comparative peace at home: for certainly the spirit of continental Europe late into the nineteenth century was not such as to encourage women to take an active part in national life. Colonel Maude preserves for us a military chorus which he says is characteristic of the spirit of pre-seventy times. It runs:

> So leben wir, so leben wir, so leben wir alle
> da;
> Des Morgens bei dem Brantwein, des
> Mittags bei dem Bier,
> Des Abends bei der Maedle in die Nacht
> Quartier.[96]

His comment is instructive: 'It may be imagined what a cheery time the smart, well set-up soldier was able to provide for himself, at the expense of anxious matrons, and particularly of housekeepers.' In fact the cheeriness of it was all-pervasive: and we can even detect a touch of pride in the Colonel's further testimony that 'the civilian had no chance in the competition for women compared with the soldier, nor could he always keep one even after he had married her.'

The Case of Finland

And as in England so in other countries where martial needs have been less pressing and martial ideals less potent. The status of women is highest in those European countries which by position or circumstance have been free from the desire or necessity of straining every nerve for imperialist or defensive ends. And, other things being equal, the converse also holds. Take the case of Finland, 'one of the happiest, most enlightened, and prosperous countries in Northern Europe,' as Mr Dover Wilson[97] described her at the end of 1914. In Finland men and women have equal rights, and on the page opposite to that on which her virtues are recorded the same author remarks quite casually: 'Without army, court, or aristocracy, and consequently without the traditions which these institutions carry with them, she presents the greatest imaginable contrasts to the Empire with which she is irrevocably linked.' Here in a word we have the main cause of Finland's progress. Is it true that her fate is irrevocably sealed?

The same facts may be observed elsewhere, and already the women of the United States and of New Zealand are beginning to realise what they owe to the peace their countries have enjoyed and to the absence of those Armies and Navies which so many would like to see them possess. Mrs Archibald Colquhoun tells us, in her vigorous attack on feminism, *The Vocation of Woman*,[98] that she has 'heard an eminent Colonial ex-statesman, who is a prominent supporter of votes for women, base his argument on the hypothesis that we have as an Imperial race passed through the stage of acquisition, in which man must play a predominant part, and are now in the stage of organisation where the sexes are equal.' If this were indeed assured the future of women would be bright indeed, but there are other voices. Listen to that of Mr Sinclair Kennedy in his recent book advocating the federation of the English-speaking peoples as a world power, *The Pan-Angles*.[99] It is thus that he speaks of America whose women owe so much to the peace their country has enjoyed: 'We *think* we are a peaceful people and deprecate as bad form the huge expenditures made by European nations for military and naval preparations. Some Americans contemplate their small army as though their nation were by that proved virtuous, much as though the learned Babu, contemplating the fur-clad Eskimo should pride himself on his own tropical attire. Like the sons of wealthy shopkeepers who disdain to demean themselves by trading, we Pan-Angles *forget sometimes on what harsh foundations was laid our present exemption from harshness.'*

And for the future, he declares, the harshness is again inevitable: though the writer admits that social progress (including of course female suffrage, which he does not mention) is largely due to peace. 'Since the throes of the eighteenth century, North America has been developed, and Australia and New Zealand have prepared themselves for large populations — *all undisturbed by fear of invasions. In these newer countries have been nurtured many of the ideals of the race* ... And it is well for us that this reign of peace has continued so long ... because of the strength it allows to accumulate for struggles to come. That this long peace is unusual, *that struggles will come, history teaches.'* The italics, as above, are ours and they serve to make clear the fate which awaits these ideals that peace has nurtured — a fate towards which in our blindness we may easily allow them to drift.

War and Population

There are many causes which underlie the contentions here set forth, but there is one consideration in particular of such primary importance that it ought not to be omitted from any historical study. 'Time was and still is,' says Olive Schreiner,[100] 'amongst almost all primitive and savage folk, when the first and all-important duty of the female to her society was to bear much and to bear unceasingly!' The welfare of

127

the tribe or of the nation has clearly depended in warlike ages on the number of adult males capable of bearing arms that it could mobilise for every tribal or national emergency. The ceaseless destruction wrought by war or acts of personal violence, and the decimating ravages of the pestilence or famine which these wars generally brought in their train, made it all important that woman should employ her creative power to its very uttermost limits if the race were not to dwindle and die out. 'May thy wife's womb never cease from bearing' is still today the highest expression of good will on the part of a native African chief to his departing guest.

This state of affairs prevailed throughout the ancient world with few exceptions, and throughout the Middle Ages, and down almost to our own day the demand for continuous, unbroken child-bearing on the part of the woman as her loftiest social duty has been hardly less imperious. Martin Luther wrote: 'If a woman becomes weary or at last dead from bearing, that matters not; let her only die from bearing, she is there to do it.' There was no dissentient voice, and the militarist ideal of a fruitful nation which should overrun its enemies by sheer force of numbers, has remained down to the present day. In theory the demand has ceased; in theory we accept the warning of Malthus; in theory we point to emigration as the sign and the remedy of overpopulation. But in fact the ideals of militarism remain the same. Think of the finger of scorn which was pointed at the prudent working classes of France by their military neighbours. It is in tones of triumph that Bernhardi turns arithmetician.[101] 'No further increase in these figures (a total army of 2,300,000) is possible, since in France 90 per cent of all those liable to serve have been called up, and the birth-rate is steadily sinking.' So France herself felt. And instead of asking how far such

128

decrease was wise from a social as opposed to a military point of view, the world calmly assumed that the day of France was over. She had decided no longer to continue in the struggle to provide food for cannon. She had put the question of social well-being first in the scale. Therefore her hour had come. And in every country this dread of being left behind in the ceaseless and unconsidered production of babies, with its persistent degradation of so many women to the position of beasts of burden, leads militarist governments to oppose every effort to reduce the birth-rate. It is in vain that eugenists and social reformers alike have deplored this blind worship of numbers, regardless of quality, regardless of the social squalor which large families entail. Even in twentieth century Europe this first requirement of woman's freedom, the claim to be something more than a domestic animal, is vigorously denied by every state that is organised for war. The right to a share in controlling her own married life is still largely a privilege which has to be won. 'To stunt one's brain in order that one may bear a son does not seem to me a process essentially sacred or noble in itself,' says Miss Cicely Hamilton, in a book which is slowly creating a revolution of thought on the subject in England, 'yet millions of others have instructed their daughters in foolishness so that they, in turn, might please, marry and beget children.'[102] And Miss Hamilton rightly points out 'such improvement as has already been effected in the status of the wife and mother is to a great extent the work of the formerly contemned spinster.' And she might, had she realised it, have pointed out that the modern spinster is a product of peace in a double sense — of the peace which allowed the industrial revolution to establish both itself and the possibility of economic independence; of the peace which so far obscured the implications of war that an unmarried woman might claim her place in respectable society.

Food For Cannon

Similarly as regards Miss Hamilton's assertion that 'the various explanations which have been given for woman's existence may be narrowed down to two — her husband and her child. Male humanity has wobbled between two convictions — the one, that she exists for the entire benefit of contemporary mankind; the other, that she exists for the entire benefit of the next generation. The latter is at present the favourite. One consideration only male humanity has firmly refused to entertain — that she exists in any degree whatsoever for the benefit of herself.'[103] Here, again, she neglects to emphasise the lesson of history; for in all ages a third reason has been given for woman's existence. Militarists have openly avowed that Heaven is on the side of the big battalions, and except perhaps in very primitive ways they never imagined that the battalions in question dropped straight from Heaven itself. 'Be fruitful and multiply' has been the warrior-statesman's command, 'and conquer the earth.'

The lesson is clear enough: for everywhere people are being forced to realise the influence which militarism exerts on moral standards and in every case in a direction unfavourable to women. But hitherto feminist writers have been content to refer casually to this fundamental obstacle to the progress of their ideals. '*The service of mother,*' wrote Ellen Key in *The Woman Movement,*[104] 'must receive the honour and oblation that the state now gives to *military service*'; but no particular emphasis is laid on the false standards which militarism creates, no mention made of the interest which women, simply as women, ought to take in the furtherance of peace ideals. Yet when the war broke out Ellen Key was amongst the first to voice the horror and distress with which feminists all over the world greeted its denial of their aspirations.

It has not been that the leaders of the movement decided to concentrate first of all on political enfranchisement in order thus to exert a peaceful influence from within their nations. They have repeatedly thrown themselves into many schemes which bore only indirectly on the political ends they had in view. They have constantly written and agitated for other ideals of womanhood than those which they have kept immediately before their supporters. They neglected the danger of militarism which threatened even their own immediate ends. Olive Schreiner, for instance, in that fine passage in *Woman and Labour*, where she contrasts the ideals of man and woman in relation to war and the destruction of life, deals with one side of the question only. 'The relations of the female,' she says, 'towards the production of human life influence undoubtedly even her relation towards animal and all life. *It is a fine day, let us go out and kill something!* cries the typical male of certain races, instinctively. *There is a living thing, it will die if it is not cared for*, says the average woman, almost equally instinctively.' And she goes on to remark that 'War will pass when intellectual culture and activity have made possible to the female an equal share in the control and governance of modern national life; it will probably not pass away much sooner; its extinction will not be delayed much longer ... it is we especially, who in the domain of war, have our word to say, a word no man can say for us. It is our intention to enter into the domain of war and to labour there till in the course of generations we have extinguished it.' And in the meantime?

'For the vast bulk of humanity, probably for

131

generations to come, the instinctive antagonism of the human childbearer to reckless destruction of that which she has at so much cost produced, will be necessary to educate the race to any clear conception of the bestiality and insanity of war.'

Instinctive Antagonism Not Enough

Herein lies the error. Instinctive antagonism is not enough: for war itself constitutes the main obstacle to that equal share in the control and governance of national life which is to inaugurate the era of peace and reasonableness. If women were to apply the same argument to political enfranchisement and to rely on their instinctive antagonism to tyranny and oppression as a method of securing the vote what would be their position today? Unfortunately we must realise the value of organisation and propaganda as the necessity of modern times. We must keep a definite end in view: and side by side with the abolition of sex-inequality in the exercise of the political rights, the feminist movement must declare its active opposition to Militarism as the menace of all women in all nations. Side by side with the forces that are working actively against the perpetuation of warfare in the future women, as women, must take their part, in their own interests primarily but also for the benefit of humanity. The task may be tremendous, but success cannot be doubtful, for where the interest and the instinct of half the human race are united in a determined effort it is hard to believe that mere tradition, however bestial, will find it possible to survive. Such an effort, and not the wars against which it is directed, is the real '*indispensable necessity* of human progress.'

Chapter V

Woman's Prerogative

'We have abolished duelling between individuals, and War, which is but a duel between nations, must go. What have we to substitute for Competition? Only Co-operation.' — Miss Jane Harrison

'War is an indispensable necessity of human progress.' — Colonel F. N. Maude, C.B.

'War is a manifestation of the world-spirit in the most sublime form.' — Professor J. A. Cramb

'On this one point, and on this point almost alone, the knowledge of woman, simply as woman, is superior to that of man; she knows the history of human flesh; she knows its cost; he does not.' — Olive Schreiner

It has been said by a leading American feminist that 'In warfare, *per se*, we find maleness in its absurdest extremes.'[105] Here, we are told, is to be studied the whole gamut of basic masculinity, from the initial instinct of combat, through every form of glorious ostentation, with the loudest possible accompaniment of noise. War shows us that men are very far from the civilisation they profess, certainly; but if that were all there would be good reason for surprise that with the advent of more rational habits of thought and action such methods of settling disputes have not long ago

133

passed into oblivion. But that is not all, and it is precisely on our understanding this fact that the hopes of the future are based.

War is the prerogative of man in a special sense, and it is because he feels this so strongly that the difficulty of gaining a hearing for views which tend fundamentally to disparage the value of war is so great. For to men war involves that element of sacrifice, of giving up one's life for others in a noble cause, that has made argument with the martyr an impossibility in all ages. To a man it is the basest treachery that anyone should breathe a word in opposition to the cause he has undertaken to defend. To do so would be to minimise the chances of success, to weaken the something which gives him driving power, and to encourage the warriors against whom he is pitted. Hence it is that as far as men are concerned it is impossible to conceive the hypothesis, so long as war lasts, that one's own side may not be entirely in the right; and hence it is that the realisation of the true position of one's adversary which might so often lead to an early cessation of hostilities is inconceivable to each and all of the nations concerned in any struggle.

But the spirit of sacrifice involves more than the unflinching course from which the martyr must look neither to the right hand nor to the left. It involves an enthusiasm which no amount of argument can overcome: a denial of self which it would be unjust to depreciate. To obey the call of King and Country is to many a duty as sacred as that a man should lay down his life for a friend: it is superior to reason: it can brook no counter considerations. In a word, as far as man is concerned the outbreak of war implies the immediate closing of every opening through which the possibility of a rapprochement might contrive to enter, and the war is left to pursue its horrible course unless some powerful neutral intervenes to separate the embittered combatants — an improbable and dangerous proceeding. All works with the inevitability of fatalism, and any suggestion of a possible alternative is regarded as the highest treason.

Meanwhile the millions of non-combatants look on aghast. Some cheer — and these form 'public opinion': all hope their own side will win, for in case of victory they will at least come in for the minimum of personal misfortune and share in the honour and glory — and in the pickings. It would be high treason, as aforesaid, to do otherwise, for that is the male code of honour in war time. *And in war time only men matter*.

Such, at any rate, has been the view hitherto: and to a large extent such is the view today. It is true that in primitive times warfare frequently had as its ultimate object the capture of females; but, for all that, women in war time are a negligible factor. They just lapse, except for camp problems, and in so far as something must be found for some of them to do. Men must preserve a discreet silence: what women say or think nobody really cares. It is a terrible confession, *yet this is a prerogative of woman of which she may well be proud today*.

It is terrible, yet it is the symbol and token of woman's greatness. She has neither part nor share in the slaughter of humanity, and *she* may speak where *man* dare not. In the past she had no voice to raise: she was not conscious of her power. Today, if she will but realise it, the redemption of civilisation rests with her, and perhaps with her alone. Woman has but to become conscious of her power, of her privilege; has but to realise that after all more than half the world, were *every* nation at war, is permanently non-combatant; and that now, when so many nations are looking on at the carnage in amazement and horror,

135

the value of public opinion is all-important. There is no question here of stopping the *present* war immediately, but of the attitude of mind which may in the near future make war an impossibility, and may even now hasten the end of this war or enable the final settlement to be in the direction of lasting peace.

For in this question men are by nature, by habit, and by tradition powerless to act, for the reasons we have set forth, and the latest and greatest confession of failure is to be found in that giant of European thought, to whom France today looks as her spiritual leader — the author of *Jean Christophe*. Solitary and despairingly, Romain Rolland,[106] in an article in the *Journal de Genève*, raises his voice above the tumult of battle in his noble appeal. 'O young men,' he cries to the young French conscripts, and joins to them in his generous sympathy the youth of all nations, friend and foe, 'O young men that shed your blood with so generous a joy! O heroism of the world! What a harvest for destruction to reap! Young men of all nations, brought into conflict by a common ideal, making enemies of those who should be brothers; all of you marching to your death are dear to me.'

The supreme sacrifice of man! And before his eyes there pass the armies of those to whom he had been as a father-confessor, the interpreter of their dreams, the poet of their highest imaginings. 'Slavs hastening to the aid of your race; Englishmen fighting for honour and right; intrepid Belgians who dared to oppose the Teutonic colossus, and defend against him the Thermopylae of the West; Germans fighting to defend the philosophy and the birthplace of Kant against the Cossack avalanche; and you, above all, my young compatriots, in whom the generation of heroes of the Revolution lives again; you, who for years have confided your dreams to me, and now, on the verge of battle, bid me a sublime farewell.'

And what have their elders done for these young men, what ideal has set them one against another? 'A maddened Europe ascending its funeral pyre, and, like Hercules, destroying itself with its own hands.' Such is the final achievement of man: pell-mell they rush on one another — souls and bodies of all colours.

'Is our civilisation so solid that you do not fear to shake the pillars on which it rests? Can you not see that all falls in upon you if one column be shattered? Could you not have learned to love one another, or, if that were impossible, at least to tolerate the great virtues and the great vices of the others? Was it not your duty to attempt — you have never attempted it in sincerity — to settle amicably the questions which divided you — the problem of peoples annexed against their will, the equitable division of productive labour and the riches of the world? Must the stronger for ever darken the others with the shadow of his pride, and the others for ever unite to dissipate it? Is there no end to this bloody and puerile sport, in which the partners change about from century to century — no end, until the whole of humanity is exhausted thereby?' And then Rolland begins his burning indictment. He confesses it. We are all to blame. 'Again the venerable refrain is heard: "The fatality of war is stronger than our wills." The old refrain of the herd that makes a god of its feebleness and bows down before him. Man has invented fate, that he may make it responsible for the disorders of the universe, those disorders which it was his duty to regulate. There is no fatality! The only fatality is what we desire; and more often, too, what we do not desire enough. Let each now repeat his *mea culpa*. The leaders of thought, the Church, the Labour parties did not desire war. That may be; what, then, did they do to prevent it? What are they doing to put an end to it? They are stirring up the bonfire, each one bringing his faggot ... There is not one amongst the leaders of thought in each country who does not proclaim with conviction that the cause of his people is the cause of God, the cause of liberty, and of human progress. And I, too, proclaim it.'

Rolland against Hauptmann![107] Yes: we all read it aghast. And here comes Rolland, repentant as it were, seeking with whom he may join hands. Labour has failed. Christianity has worse than failed: it has denied itself. 'You Christians today would not have refused to sacrifice to the gods of Imperial Rome; you are not capable of such courage. You also are undismayed by bullets and shrapnel yet tremble before the dictates of racial frenzy — that Moloch that stands higher than the Church of Christ.' *Et propter vitam, vivendi perdere causas!*[108] But worse than this is the unutterable despair of his fellow-men which drives Rolland to his final confession of all. There is none left to hear! 'I know that such thoughts have little chance of being heard today. Young Europe, lusting for battle, will smile contemptuously and show its fangs like a young wolf.' It is a useless struggle! He speaks merely for the sake of speaking. 'I do not speak to convince others, I speak but to solace my own conscience.'

Thus the greatest mind of Europe — the supreme message of man to man, A.D. 1914. There is none to hear! 'I speak but to solace my own conscience!' Young men, old men, working-men, diplomatists, priests, imperialists — they will not hear. *But it is always of men he thinks.* Not a mention of women, of the women that hear him gladly, in whose hearts his words find a ready echo, his noble words: 'Our duty it is to rise above tempests, and thrust aside the clouds; to build higher and stronger, dominating the injustice and hatred of nations, the walls of that city wherein the souls of the whole world may assemble.'

This is the cry that women may take up: the cry that men will not and dare not hear. To such ideals the press of all the world is closed, the platforms of all the world are silent. But in print and in speech women may already help forward these ideals, and none will say them nay. For the times have changed, but the nature of woman cannot change, as some of her enemies have most truly declared. Woman, because to her has fallen the task of bringing into the world those human souls and bodies which in war are but food for cannon, is able to realise what man is not able. 'For such a purpose,' she might well say now that she has attained self-consciousness, 'I will not bring more human life into the world.' And man would neither understand nor would he be greatly shocked. It matters not to him what women are saying or thinking, for women are but women.

Yet a public opinion must be created, and how can that be if the voice that is privileged fails to make itself heard? 'Women of all nations unite!'; that should be the new cry − not 'Woman has *no* country!' but 'Woman must have every country!' and whoever raises such a cry may be sure that it will not solace an individual conscience alone. Such a cry, already heard, though in far-off muffled tones, in every branch of the women's movement, must wake an echo in the hearts of millions who will pass it on to others. It will not seem treachery to a cause: it will not seem the coward's mean appeal; for it will be but the voice of Nature driven to rebellion by the horrors of violence and destruction. Not that woman has yet realised her mission of peace, the privilege that her imagined weakness has bestowed. Many women, perhaps most women, are still caught in the meshes in which the tradition of long years of subjection has enveloped them. They gaze blindly at the carnage or hasten to staunch the blood that flows — as ministering angels, to heal the wounds that the heroism of man has dealt to his brother. And rightly, for this is their duty in such a time. But it is clearly not enough to be content to do one's duty here. The blood flows too fast, it is only some drops that are staunched — the wounds gape too wide, it is only the scratches that are healed; and meanwhile the bodies are piled higher and higher, the graves are dug deeper and deeper.

But if woman climbed up to the clearer air above the battlefield and cried aloud in her anguish to her sisters afar off: 'These things must not be, they shall never be again!' would man indeed say, 'Down with her!'? Would he not allow her prerogative? Would he not even wish to climb up, too?

Yet it is not on this note that we would conclude, for the issues involved reach far beyond the present, with its trials and its dilemmas. Whatever may be possible at the moment, it is clear that on these issues depends the whole future of woman. When peace is finally declared, whether through the exercise of her prerogative or because the destructive energies of man shall have spent their force, a new international organisation must be formed. It must weld together in its higher ideal — the substitution of co-operation and understanding for violence between nations — the groups which nationally, and even within each nation, are split asunder by diverse conditions, by method, and by language. The practical next steps must be the concern of others. Ours has been the humbler task of strengthening their arguments and of rousing their less active supporters.

Extracts from Militarism, Feminism
and the Birthrate

Chapter II

The Nature of the Case

The antithesis between Militarism and Feminism is not only emphasised throughout history in every age and country but it is inherent in the very nature of things.

In history it is for the most part war itself that we can study, but war is only one of the evils which can be grouped under [the] conception of militarism. War is but the outward sign of the military spirit, just as the demand for the vote is often the most visible manifestation of the feminist movement.

But militarism is first and foremost a system. It may appear in its extremest forms with a small armament, or be present only in the background with a large one, as in England. 'It is militarism when a European king always wears a military uniform. It represents an idea ... This is a way of looking at State affairs, and it colours everything else. Therefore it is militarism when military officers despise civilians ... It is militarism when railroads are built as military strategy requires, not as trade requires' ... Of every new invention militarism asks: How can it be rendered useful for military purposes? ... Militarism is also a philosophy and temper which is accordant with imperialism. It consists in aggression and domination instead of conciliation and concession. It is militarism to "jam things through" without consideration for the feelings and interests of other people, except so far as they can strike back, whether it is done in a legislature or on the field of battle.'[1]

Chapter X

The Latest Phase

When the European conflict had been in progress a few months it seemed well to put on record the hopes and fears of those who adopt the position which the present volume is designed to support; and as a result the following was contributed to *Jus Suffragii* and appeared in the issue of February 1915:[2]

Since the outbreak of the war many women have been almost afraid to ask themselves what will be the ultimate result of the European upheaval on the movement for which so many of them have sacrificed almost all they had to give in the past ten years — their time, their energy, and their resources. It has seemed to them too narrow, too selfish a question to raise in an emergency which deafened the peoples of Europe to every appeal but the call to arms, when their very existence was at stake in face of the ruin which the armies of destruction bring in their train, — when the youth and chivalry of the nations were devoting themselves with unexampled heroism to the cause they believed to be right, when every home was mourning for someone near and dear, some friendship lost, some brave career brought to an untimely end. How could one longer put forward the claims of a fraction, of a minority, in face of the peril and need of all?

But whatever may have been the case at first, we may now surely pause to take breath and ask, Is this diffidence any longer necessary? Must not women in justice to themselves face the hard facts? And when those facts are faced, does not a policy which advocates continued advance on the old and well-known lines open up a prospect so black as to drive the boldest to despair? At any rate, it is such that all who can do anything to save what little there is that makes for honour, for freedom, and for justice from the wreckage which strews the path of the warriors of Europe, are called upon to exert themselves to the utmost to save that little, and to oppose the reign of unreason by which civilisation is threatened. At any rate, it is time for those whose ideals have been the ideals of peace, of co-operation and construction to come forward and assert their claim to be heard, lest in the universal madness that has overcome mankind all chance of realising any of those ideals be lost for generations, or as some are urging, for ever. It is time to suggest that there are some things worse than warfare itself, and those who will first realise it are the women of all nations.

Slowly, slowly, through the centuries the bestial in humanity had been taught to take a lower place: slowly mankind had come to understand that war is not the only end of education and of life: slowly the idea of dwelling together in unity, and of the social well-being of all had raised its head upon the earth. And at length woman, whose function in life is the negation of the spirit of repression and destruction that had ruled throughout the ages, realised that with her lay the future of the race. Her awakening was the consummation of the long struggle for freedom by the slave and the oppressed; her ideal the ideal of peace, of construction, and of co-operation: and slowly, slowly, that idea for which she was fighting so earnestly had begun to redeem the race from barbarism.

In some countries she had won an equal share with man in the direction of human affairs: and these are perhaps not by chance even now the countries of peace! Soon it seemed she might win a similar influence in other lands, and the wars that man spoke of as inevitable might have been banished from the terrors of the world.

But the evil day came too soon, a very little too soon, only a very little. What is past cannot be undone; the torrent has been let loose, and the hope of a better and nobler spirit has been suddenly dashed to the ground. Well nigh in vain it seems did the Christ live upon the earth, and well nigh in vain have the brave women laboured who toiled so long and so hard for the truth that was in them.

Let us make no mistake: *the forces of violence and ruin threaten us as never before in human history*, for our stake is greater. No Xerxes, no Attila, was a menace more terrible than the spirit of hatred and cruelty, the era of man-made law, that threatens to be the legacy of this conflict. Let us not deceive ourselves, *the emancipation of women is more remote today, unless women organise to meet the new situation, than it has been for many a century*.

And the reason for this is clear to all who have studied the Suffrage movement and its opponents with any regard for what lies even just below the surface. The Suffrage movement has been essentially the movement of peace, relying for its success on the growth of the peace idea, and denying the assertion that the government of peoples can be based any longer on physical force. So long as the warrior spirit prevailed, so long as every man lived in terror of his neighbour, and groups of neighbours in equal terror of other fighting groups within fighting distance — so long did man, the hunter, the warrior, egotist, the destroyer, bend everything to his will. The safety of all demanded it. And as long as Europe remains an armed camp inspired by the bitterness of rankling hatred and revenge, so long will woman the sympathetic, the unanimist, the creator, be forced to bow down to his will, to yield to the all-conquering argument of physical force. Even before the war the great majority were only half converted to the new ideal; and when the storm burst they soon assigned to woman her proper sphere. She must bandage, she must sew, she must keep things going at home, she may pray, she may weep — while they go forth to do the work of the world, to destroy their thousands and their ten thousands. But when they are pleased to return from their triumphs woman may find that to bandage and sew, to pray and weep, is not a privilege which entitles her to an equal share in the affairs of the nation; men will once again manage all things, except the baby, until the next war comes. If the 'no-nonsense' argument, the argument that Imperial affairs are not women's affairs, that grave matters of national policy involving the risk of armed aggressions must be in the hands of strong, silent men, was at the back of so many minds before the war, then now that war has broken out it will be a thousandfold stronger, with all that this implies. In other words, the movement *for women's enfranchisement supported solely by the old arguments from 'rights' and 'needs' on a national basis is no longer sufficient to meet the new situation.* It can no longer suffice of itself to arouse an enthusiasm worthy of the great battle that the women of the whole world will now have to fight in common. It is madness to go on only in the same old way: stupidity to imagine that of itself this war will inaugurate an era of peace and justice, folly even to point to the breaking down of old barriers, and the new work that women have taken on themselves in time of war. The old prejudices will be entrenched more strongly than ever; the new work may be found to be a sop thrown contemptuously to inferior creatures, merely because men for the time being had more important business in hand.

Is then the vote, the highest symbol to women of that ultimate social recognition she has been striving for, an utter impossibility during the lifetime of those who are growing up full of hope and anxious to do their share in the reconstruction that must come? By no means — if only women will meet the changed situation with promptitude and determination; if only they will realise that the opposition to their ideals comes from the evils of nationalism: not from the nationalism which assists in preserving valuable characteristics and traditions in the service of humanity, but the evil nationalism which is artificially maintained by an envenomed press with its empty catchwords of hate, fraught with the power to hurl innocent industrious folk one against the other in the vain belief that either can be the ultimate gainer.

There is no place for women's true work in a world divided by the frenzy of social hatred, suspicious, revengeful, and unrestrainable. The people of such a Europe would have little to distinguish them morally from those wild beasts whereat we point in their captivity as a sign that mankind have progressed — save the absence of a force mightier than they to fit bars to the national cages which alone might keep them from flying at one another's throats.

But if women realise this, if they grasp the new significance of internationalism, the future is bright with hope. For the future lies with those social movements which can work on an international basis. No one country will dare to lead the way in such a matter, where all are suspicious of all. Hitherto women have been organised not only nationally but in bickering groups within a nation. Henceforward a larger aim must unite them in their opposition to the forces of violence and reaction. On all main principles women are really united, as is shown by the unanimity with which the leaders of the movement in all lands have condemned the frenzy which in their purely national associations they were powerless to check. And now while national societies must be kept alive for the necessary work they have to do — how necessary is shown in England by the degrading episodes at Plymouth and Cardiff[3] only a few weeks ago — all energetic endeavours must centre *on the creation of an international organisation which may gather together such sane opinion as is left in the world and render it articulate*. Meanwhile let every woman think on this, and remember that a day will come when those frenzied beasts to which the great nations of Europe may now be likened, will sink back exhausted from the struggle: in that day it will be her duty to join with those who are preparing to seize them firmly by the tails and insert a ring of peace through their noses, and lead them to a world where the diplomatist and the diplodocus[4] may lie down together as a symbol of evil days that are past — under the same gravestone.

Chapter XII

The Prevention of War

Every suffragist society ought to be a pacifist society and realise that pacifist propaganda is an integral part of suffrage propaganda. — Mrs H. M. Swanwick

One of the most depressing lessons of recent events is the unlikelihood that men of themselves will ever take active steps in sufficient numbers to combat the madness of international pugnacity. But those who despair are chiefly content to think in terms of men alone. The alternative ideal certainly demands no little effort on the part of all interested in its realisation. That women should actively concern themselves with peace is however no new thing, though their motives for such concern have certainly been very various ... [There follows the historical survey referred to earlier — Ed.]

The time has now come for more definite organisation on a world wide basis, and for a fuller enumeration of the obstacles to be surmounted and the means of achieving the end in view.

First of all as regards the psychological causes of war. Mrs Swanwick in her pamphlet *Women and War* has classified them as follows:

151

(1) A traditional conception of honour and the belief that it can be 'vindicated' by force.
(2) Love of gain and the drive of vested interests.
(3) Love of domination and what is often called glory.
(4) Fear.

These motives are the mainspring of Governments, but they could not work the war-machine if, in the mass of men, there were strong resistance, and, indeed, if there were not, in the mass of men, other motives, which may be roughly classed as:

(5) Indolence of mind, which leaves all thinking and planning to those whose vested interests may advantage from war.
(6) Pugnacity.
(7) Love of hazard and adventure and disgust with the drabness of daily life.

It is these motives and instincts on which the war-mongers play. Today they are directed into the channels of militarism chiefly through the two great media of the Press and Education.

With the perversion of Education by war we have already dealt,[5] and here the counteraction of military influences is the special task of women. In particular, of course, an attack must be made on the prevailing conception of history — the false emphasis on military exploits, the narrow view of patriotism, the paeans in honour of the glory of war.

But of even more immediate urgency is the problem of the Press, with which we may deal in greater detail. For one of the main lessons of the war for all who are concerned with the advancement of ideals such as those we have been discussing, is the supreme value of an efficient press organisation during the time of crisis. More and more it is becoming evident that the influence of the press is paramount in the formation of public opinion, and the frequent re-iteration of doctrines however pernicious, in posters, headlines or leaders is too often sufficient to overbear the secret aspirations of all but the most hardened idealist. We begin by taking a paper for its news and we end by succumbing to the atmosphere with which that news is invested ... We are concerned here with the relations of the press to matters militarist, and to the bearing of those relations on the future of the women's movement.

The inclusion of the press amongst the institutions which at present make for war is today a regrettable necessity. The position has been summed up by Principal Graham,[6] in language which admits of no improvement: 'Then there are the newspapers. War time is their harvest ... The subject is exciting of itself, and easy to write about. To pander to the street excitement endears a writer to the crowd. Popularity comes to the patriot editor whose armchair is the seat of war. Every paper which fights for peace, does so to its financial loss in just the days dangerous to the maintenance of peace ... We all have a duty to support the papers of the peacemakers.'

The moral of all this is obvious and suggests the wording of that supplementary resolution which should be moved again and again till its object has been achieved: 'The need for securing and supporting a press which shall fearlessly put forward the ideals of the International Women's Movement now for the first time conscious of its task, and shall serve as a centre of activity, and a means of propaganda, encouragement and intercommunication.'[7]

If women have a point of view of their own in every matter of social interest, the application of this ad-mission to those international affairs which constantly overshadow the more immediate preoccupations of the social reformer, renders doubly imperative the necessity of establishing a really permanent international platform for the expression of this point of view . . . this is where the need for a special Women's organisation is immediately apparent.

* * *

At the head of the final chapter of the manuscript, a quotation is inserted, which seems to sum up the beliefs and the hopes of the authors and also the growing consciousness of feminist pacifists in 1915. It is from a report which appeared in the *Manchester Guardian* on 20 April 1915, of a meeting to approve the programme for the Hague congress. In seconding the resolution of approval, Maude Royden[8] said that

. . . the vast mass of the women of the country were only waiting for a lead to perceive that peace and the women's movement went together. War was the women's worst enemy, and it affected the whole position of women as a sex. The advance of civilisation depended on their realisation of the fact that men and women were not, and could not be, governed by violence, but only by spiritual force. Everywhere where there was pacifism the women's movement advanced; everywhere where there was militarism it went back.

Notes

Introduction

1   For example, Helena M. Swanwick, *Women and War* and *War in Its Effect on Women* (London, 1915, reprinted New York: Garland, 1971); J.A. Hobson, *Toward International Government* (London 1915, reprinted New York: Garland, 1971); C.R. Buxton, ed, *Towards a Lasting Settlement* (London, 1915, reprinted New York: Garland, 1971). Leonard Woolf also wrote in 1915 two reports on international government, which appeared in the *New Statesman* in July 1915, and later as a book.

2   Catherine E. Marshall (1880–1961), suffragist, pacifist, internationalist. See below, pp. 7–20. Marshall left an extensive collection of papers, which found their way to the Cumbria Record Office in 1962, where the present writer (J.V.) did the primary sorting in 1969 and 1975–78. J.V. is writing Marshall's biography. See Jo Vellacott, *Bertrand Russell and the Pacifists in the First World War* (Brighton: Harvester Press, 1980; New York: St Martin's Press, 1981); Jo Vellacott, 'Feminist Consciousness and the First World War' in Ruth Roach Pierson and Somer Broadribb, eds, *Women and Peace: Theoretical, Historical and Practical Perspectives* (forthcoming, London: Croom Helm, 1987), also forthcoming in *History Workshop Journal*, No. 23. See also Jo Vellacott Newberry, 'Antiwar Suffragists', *History*, Vol. 62, October 1977.

3   There were a number of important suffrage organisations of which the best-known are the Women's Social and Political Union, militant 'suffragettes', dominated by Christabel and Emmeline Pankhurst; and the National Union of

Women's Suffrage Societies, non-militant suffragists, 'constitutionalists', of which Millicent Fawcett (see note 36) was President. The terms 'militant' and 'non-militant' are somewhat misleading, since both societies were extremely active and visible, although the NUWSS stayed strictly within the law, and did not seek confrontation.

4   See, in addition to British works, e.g. Eleanor Flexner's excellent *Century of Struggle: the Woman's Rights Movement in the United States* (Cambridge, Mass. and London: Harvard University Press, rev. 1975); Catherine Cleverdon, *The Women's Suffrage Movement in Canada* (Toronto, 1950, 1974).

5   Helena M. Swanwick (1864–1939), journalist, pacifist and feminist author. One of the early women students at Cambridge. Founding member of the UDC, first chair of the Women's International League (1915), the British wing of what was to become the Women's International League for Peace and Freedom. First British woman delegate to the League of Nations Assembly (1924). Her autobiography *I Have Been Young* (London: Gollancz, 1935) deserves to be better known.

6   Margaret Kamester, 'The Secondary Feminist interests of the WSPU and the NUWSS, as found in their journals for the period January 1, 1914 to August 4, 1914'. Unpublished paper, 1982.

7   May Wright Sewall (1844–1920), United States teacher, suffragist, internationalist, pacifist. Founding member of American National Council of Women and of the International Council of Women and influential in the work of these in peace education. Sailed to Europe on Henry Ford's peace ship, 1915. Maintained her stand against war even after US intervention in 1917, when pacifism became unpopular.

8   Something of the same semi-voluntary dissociation of causes had taken place in Britain over the campaign for repeal of the Contagious Diseases Acts, while the close identification in the minds of at least the liquor industry between temperance and the women's vote in the USA was to prove a real threat to enfranchisement (Flexner, *op. cit.*).

9   Sandi Cooper, 'Women's Participation in European Peace Movements: The Struggle to Prevent World War I', in Pierson and Broadribb, *op. cit.*, which contains several useful articles on pre-war feminist pacifism; also Lela B. Costin, 'Feminism, Pacifism, Internationalism and the 1915

International Congress of Women', *Women's Studies International Forum*, Vol. 5, No. 3/4, 1982, whose view differs from Cooper's in denying importance to the women's pre-war role in peace organisations.

10   Henry Noel Brailsford (1873—1958), socialist, journalist, author, historian, keen and creative supporter of women's suffrage, he helped promote first the Conciliation Bills and later the EFF. Author of *The War of Steel and Gold*, published in 1914 before the war broke out. Active in UDC.

11   Philip Snowden (1864—1937), socialist MP, a major figure in the British Labour movement. Wrote and spoke in favour of women's suffrage, opposed the war, championed conscientious objectors.

12   James Keir Hardie (1856—1915), miner, trade unionist, journalist, MP, initially a strong supporter of the WSPU, and always a suffragist. Pacifist internationalist socialist for whom war was unthinkable.

13   George Lansbury (1859—1940), Labour MP, Christian socialist, pacifist. Gave up his seat in 1912 in order to fight a by-election on a women's suffrage platform; he lost. After 1914, editor of the socialist *Daily Herald*.

14   Bertrand Russell (1872—1970), British philosopher, prolific writer on moral and social issues. He was a strong opponent of the First World War and, at Catherine Marshall's instigation, worked full time for the No Conscription Fellowship from 1916 to early 1918, when he was imprisoned for a written comment hostile to the US. Later noted for his role in the CND (Campaign for Nuclear Disarmament), which again led to a short imprisonment in 1961. Generally, a pragmatic pacifist rather than an absolute one, but committed to work, at whatever personal cost, for the preservation of the world.

15   By 1917, adult suffrage had become politically a viable possibility. Before the war, it was rejected by the majority of serious supporters of women's suffrage because of the apparent unlikelihood of acceptance of such a broad measure; accordingly most suffrage societies held to the campaign for the women's vote 'on the same terms as it is or may be given to men'. For working-class women's support of this limited objective see Jill Liddington and Jill Norris, *One Hand Tied Behind Us* (London: Virago Press, 1978) and Jill Liddington, *The Life and Times of a Respectable Rebel: Selina Cooper, 1864—1946* (London: Virago Press, 1984).

16   W.G. Rimmer, *Marshalls of Leeds, Flaxspinners* (Cambridge:

Cambridge University Press, 1960), traces the story of Catherine's paternal family, which was a classic example of the making of a modest fortune during the Industrial Revolution, followed by land purchase and moving away from the business roots.

17 From childhood, Marshall suffered from severe headaches which also seem to have been the main symptom of bouts of serious illness in adulthood.

18 Kathleen D. Courtney (1878–1974), Honorary Secretary of the NUWSS, later Dame Kathleen Courtney.

19 Not only have the non-militants not received their share of historical attention, but the pre-war radicals within the NUWSS were 'forgotten' by the NU's own historians (principally Millicent Fawcett and Ray Strachey) after the controversies of 1915 left their legacy of hurt feelings. Those who supported the war were those who later wrote the histories. Ray Strachey, *Millicent Garrett Fawcett* (London, 1931) and *The Cause* (London, 1928; reprinted London: Virago Press, 1978); M.G. Fawcett, *The Women's Victory and After* (London, 1920) and *What I Remember* (London, 1924). Correspondence in the possession and seen by courtesy of Frank Marshall also refers.

20 The EFF campaign never had a chance to test its potential. By-elections in 1913 and 1914 had seemed to show some promising results, but the General Election expected for 1915 was postponed because of the war.

21 Sir Edward Grey, Viscount Grey of Fallodon (1862–1933), British Foreign Secretary, 1905–16. Despite constant pressure from the NUWSS and his own convictions, Grey had never made women's suffrage a priority over other political considerations. See e.g. Leslie Parker Hume, *The National Union of Women's Suffrage Societies, 1897–1914* (New York and London: Garland, 1982) *passim*.

22 'Notes of private interview with Sir E. Grey', 15 December 1913, Marshall Papers. Emphasis Marshall's. The comparison between women and 'natives' was also used (pejoratively) by anti-suffragists. See Brian Harrison, *Separate Spheres* (London: Croom Helm, 1978).

23 Vellacott, *Bertrand Russell*, ch. 2 refers. For an illuminating view of Liberal press opinion, see Irene Cooper Willis, *England's Holy War* (New York: Garland, 1971, first published in three parts 1919–21).

24 Selina Cooper (1864–1946), born in Cornwall, moved to Lancashire when young and worked as child labourer in a

cotton factory. Never one to accept conditions unquestioningly, she became politically involved as a young woman, active in women's suffrage and trade unionism, and an elected local government representative. Worked as paid organiser for the NUWSS. Her commitment to peace was actively pursued throughout the rest of her life. See Liddington, *op. cit.*

25 Although the parallel is far from exact because of the disparity in age and status, the present writer (J.V.), thinking of this experience, remembers spending much of August 1939, as a schoolgirl, taking part in a League of Nations Union summer school in Geneva and returning home to find that all our serious discussion of routes to a peaceful world had been a fantasy without a future; everything we had discussed was irrelevant.

26 This also indicates that the organisational and political skills of the NUWSS had won admiration and respect, however grudging, before the war — an important point in light of the myth that the vote was granted only after the war revealed women's abilities.

27 I (J.V.) have not been able to find out if this was paid work.

28 Correspondence in Marshall Papers refers.

29 This has long been my (J.V.'s) view, based mainly on anecdotal references in correspondence and other suggestive evidence which it is impossible to quantify. What is certain is that as the war went on, opinion was increasingly polarised, with a growing dissent among some workers and a more determined suppression of criticism on the part of the government. T.C. Kennedy, 'Public Opinion and the Conscientious Objector, 1915–1919', *Journal of British Studies*, Vol. XII, No. 2, May 1973, examines one aspect of this question, concluding that majority opinion was strongly against the COs; the fact remains that there may have been a great deal of unarticulated uneasiness, especially after the rejection of German peace feelers in December 1916. 1917 saw substantial industrial unrest.

30 For the UDC, see H.M. Swanwick, *Builders of Peace* (London: Swarthmore Press, 1924); Marvin Swartz, *The Union of Democratic Control* (London: Oxford University Press, 1971).

31 I.C. Willis, *op. cit.*, argues that the Liberal Party, supposedly internationalist and committed to principle, had more need of Hun-hating propaganda (to create the illusion of the Holy War, to which the title of her book refers) than the Conservatives might have had, who believed war to be a

respectable way of solving international differences.

32 Mary Sheepshanks (1872–1958), secretary of the IWSA and editor of *Jus Suffragii* 1913–19. Feminist, pacifist and internationalist. For her full story see Sybil Oldfield, *Spinsters of This Parish* (London: Virago Press, 1984), where the editorial is more fully quoted on pp. 180–1.

33 Marshall often made notes of interviews, and a number of these are to be found in the Marshall Papers.

34 Isabella Ford, a Quaker from Leeds, had been an active labour organiser and important in pre-war suffrage developments. She was one of relatively few members of the pre-war NUWSS executive to be associated with the Labour Party.

35 The controversy is reflected in the NUWSS Executive Minutes of the period, in letters and statements from resigning members (Fawcett Collection) and in correspondence, especially in the Marshall Papers.

36 Millicent Garrett Fawcett, later Dame Millicent Fawcett (1847–1929), had been President of the NUWSS since 1897, and involved in the struggle since 1867. She was a staunch liberal feminist, committed to women's education and women's suffrage, but was quite unable to grasp or even tolerate the viewpoint of those who wanted to work for peace in wartime. She was deeply hurt by the dispute and remained cold and unfriendly towards Marshall and Courtney in particular, refusing to see Courtney in November 1916 when she was approached through an intermediary. In October 1917 Pippa Strachey described her as still 'fearsome about the pacifists and their works' though prepared to work with the WIL towards the new Reform Bill. Correspondence seen by courtesy of Mrs Barbara Halpern.

37 Helena Auerbach, a long-time member of the NUWSS Executive, and Ray Strachey were particularly supportive of Fawcett's 'anti-pacifist' stand.

38 Aletta Jacobs (1854–1929), first woman admitted to a Dutch university and first woman doctor in the Netherlands. Followed a career as physician in Amsterdam and then a second career as President of the Dutch suffrage society. Deeply concerned with social injustice (particularly its effects on the health of women), prostitution, and the need for birth control to be made available, she was a suffragist from 1882 on. After the war, worked with WILPF for relief of the blockade, the release of German

POWs still held in Siberia, and revision of the Treaty of Versailles.

39   There was a 'secret' international gathering of socialist women held in Berne, Switzerland in March 1915, to which several leading British socialist suffragists went (*Labour Leader*, 8 April 1915). C.K. Ogden describes this as 'the gathering which led the way for the great congress of women at the Hague', which it cannot have been in any formal sense, although the extent to which women were 'on the move' is of great interest. 'Militarism, Feminism and the Birthrate', ms. ch. X, 18–19, Ogden Papers.

40   The fullest recent account is in Anne Wiltsher, *Most Dangerous Women: Feminist Peace Campaigners of the Great War* (London: Pandora Press, 1985); see also Gertrude Bussey and Margaret Tims, *The Women's International League for Peace and Freedom* (London, 1965); Jane Addams, E. Balch and A. Hamilton, *Women at the Hague* (New York, 1915; Garland reprint, 1971); Mercedes Randall, *Improper Bostonian: Emily Greene Balch* (New York, 1964). Extensive material in Marshall Papers, in WILPF archives, University of Colorado, in Swarthmore College Peace Collection, and in WIL (British section of WILPF) archives, British Library of Political and Economic Science.

41   Jane Addams (1880–1935), United States Quaker, reformer, pacifist, writer. Co-founded Hull House, Chicago, a major development in the settlement movement. Proponent of co-operation as central in the local and international response to industrialisation. President of Women's Peace Party, 1915; Chair, Hague conference, 1915; International President WILPF from its founding to 1929.

42   This is a remarkably clear and simple document describing a procedure that might have been workable; the plan uses the neutrals in a way that bypasses some of the difficulties inherent in opening negotiations. Reprinted in Addams, Balch and Hamilton, *op. cit.*

43   Quoted by Wiltsher, *op. cit.*, p. 89. For a full account of press reaction, see *Towards Permanent Peace: A Record of the Women's International Congress*, published by the British committee, 1915, pp. 20–1.

44   Bertrand Russell increasingly longed for more action, and was deeply impressed with the humanity and practicality of the women's approach, as well as their ability to communicate across national frontiers. See e.g. Russell to Ottoline

Morrell, dated Thursday 13 April 1915 (but probably 15 April; 13 April was a Tuesday). Ottoline Morrell Papers, Texas.

45 'Notes for Speeches', Marshall Papers.

46 T.C. Kennedy, *The Hound of Conscience: A History of the No Conscription Fellowship, 1914–1919* (Fayetteville: University of Arkansas, 1981); Vellacott, *Bertrand Russell*; Vellacott Newberry, 'Antiwar Suffragists'.

47 *Militarism, Feminism and the Birthrate*, ms. ch. X, pp. 18–19. Ogden papers, see n. 53.

48 *Cambridge Magazine*, 6 March 1915, p. 327. This passage corresponds to pp. 127–30 of *Militarism versus Feminism*. Other articles in the series appeared on 20 February, pp. 276–9 (cf. Chapter I), 27 February, pp. 298–301 (cf. sections of Chapter IV); and 13 March, pp. 344–9 (cf. sections of Chapters II and HI).

49 P. Sargant Florence and J.R.L. Anderson, eds, *C.K. Ogden: A Collective Memoir* (London: Elek Pemberton, 1977), p. 17.

50 I.A. Richards, 'Some Recollections of C.K. Ogden', *Encounter*, September 1957, p. 11.

51 C.K. Ogden, 'Militarism and Feminism: What War Means to Women', *Common Cause: Organ of the National Union of Women's Suffrage Societies*, 26 February 1915, p. 735.

52 M. Sargant Florence and C. K. Ogden, 'Women's Prerogative', *Jus Suffragii*, 1 January 1915, pp. 218–9 (cf. last section of Chapter V).

M. Sargant Florence and C.K. Ogden, 'Women and War: Hopes and Fears for the Future', *Jus Suffragii*, 1 February 1915, pp. 234–5 (this article is not part of *Militarism versus Feminism*, but is to be found in the manuscript of the longer version which Ogden hoped to publish – see extracts from this version, p. 145).

'Militarism versus Feminism', *Jus Suffragii*, March 1915, supplement: this is stated to be 'the joint production of several collaborators under the general direction of Mrs Sargant Florence and Mr C.K. Ogden', and consists of the greater part of Chapters IV and I of *Militarism versus Feminism*.

Jus Suffragii was the journal of the IWSA, and under the inspired editorship of Mary Sheepshanks provided a strong and uncompromising voice against militarism and for international co-operation and feminism throughout the war.

53 C.K. Ogden's papers are at McMaster University, Hamil-

ton, Ontario, in the William Ready Division of Archives and Research Collections, Mills Memorial Library. All further mentions of correspondence refer to this collection.

54 *The Times*, 23 March 1957, p. 11.

55 P. Sargant Florence and J.R.L. Anderson, eds, *op. cit.*, p. 30.

56 I.A. Richards, *op. cit.*, p. 11.

57 P. Sargant Florence and J.R.L. Anderson, eds, *op. cit.*, p. 21.

58 See letters from Maude Royden, December 1914 and February 1915, and from Helena Swanwick, March and April 1915.

59 P. Sargant Florence and J.R.L. Anderson, eds, *op. cit.*, p. 58.

60 *Ibid.*, p. 35.

61 I.A. Richards, *op. cit.*, p. 10.

62 *Ibid.*, p. 233.

63 *Ibid.*, p. 81.

64 C.K. Ogden, I.A. Richards and J. Wood, *Foundations of Aesthetics* (London: Allen & Unwin, 1922).

65 C.K. Ogden and I.A. Richards, *The Meaning of Meaning: A Study of the Influence of Language Upon Thought and of the Science of Symbolism*, International Library of Psychology, Philosophy and Scientific Method (London: Kegan Paul, 1923).

66 I.A. Richards, *op. cit.*, p. 12.

67 Thanks to Dr W. Terrence Gordon for letting us read his essay, 'Significs and C.K. Ogden; The Influence of Lady Welby', to be published in 1987, also for other information on Lady Welby.

68 Quoted by Achim Eschbach in his preface to the reprint of Victoria Lady Welby's *What is Meaning?* (Philadelphia: John Benjamins, 1983).

69 P. Sargant Florence and J.R.L. Anderson, *op. cit.*, p. 161. See also *Onwards to Victory: War Speeches by the Rt. Hon. Winston S. Churchill*, compiled by Charles Eade (Toronto: McClelland & Stewart, 1944), pp. 233–9: 'A Speech on Receiving an Honorary Degree at Harvard, September 6, 1943'.

70 See pp. 136–8 of *Militarism versus Feminism*.

71 P. Sargant Florence and J.R.L. Anderson, *op. cit.*, p. 233.

72 *The Times*, 23 March 1957, p. 11.

73 *The Times*, 16 December 1954, p. 10.

74 *The Suffrage Annual and Women's Who's Who* (London: Stanley Paul, 1913), p. 350.

75 Lella Secor Florence, *A Diary in Letters 1915–1922*, Barbara Moench Florence, ed (New York: Burt Franklin, 1978).

76 G.M. Waters, *Dictionary of British Artists Working 1900–1950* (Eastbourne: Eastbourne Fine Arts, 1975), Vol. 1, p. 116.

77 *The Suffrage Annual*, 1913, p. 350.

78 *Ibid*.

79 *Towards Permanent Peace*, p. 24.

80 Letter from Helena Swanwick to C.K. Ogden, 7 March 1915.

81 This letter is in the Bertrand Russell archives at McMaster University, Hamilton, Ontario.

82 See especially a series of articles in February 1918 by P. Tudor Hart and M. Sargant Florence.

83 *The Times*, 16 December 1954. We have to take *The Times'* word for this remarkable saying of Michelangelo.

84 The Chelsea Old Town Hall now houses the Chelsea Branch of the Royal Borough of Kensington and Chelsea Library; the four artists commissioned to decorate the main Council Chamber in 1911 were chosen in a competition which aroused the usual quota of controversy – however the panel painted by Sargant Florence seems to have been the most universally approved of the four. The panels were erected in 1914 and remain there today. Thanks to Mrs P.K. Pratt, Chelsea Branch Librarian, for this information.

   The eight frescoes by Sargant Florence are still in the Old School at Oakham, which is now a theatre, known as the Shakespeare Centre, where I saw them, and appreciate the courtesy shown me there (J.V.).

85 Mary Sargant Florence, *Colour Co-ordination* (London: John Lane, 1940).

86 M. Lowndes, 'Genius and Women Painters', *Common Cause*, 17 April 1914, p. 31.

87 L.S. Florence, *op. cit.*, p. 204.

88 *Ibid.*, p. 256, note 4.

89 *Jus Suffragii*, March 1915, supplement (see note 52, above).

90 See e.g. the extensive quotes from her 1915 pamphlet, *Women and War* in Chapter XII of *Militarism, Feminism and the Birthrate*, in Ogden's Papers, and above, pp. 151–2.

91 23 December 1914, in Ogden Papers.

92 *Times Literary Supplement*, 22 April 1915, p. 140.

93 Cecil Delisle Burns (1879–1942), a scholar and prolific writer in the fields of politics, history and philosophy. He held posts in the Ministry of Reconstruction in Britain in 1917–19, and afterwards in the Labour Office of the League of Nations.

94 Frederica Bremer (1801–65) Swedish writer and feminist.

Her 'Appeal to the Women of the World to Form an Alliance' was made in revulsion against the sufferings of the Crimean War; her vision of an international organisation of women to foster peace was called 'the mere illusion of an amiable enthusiast' (*The Times*, 28 August 1854). A modern evaluation, however, speaks of her 'pioneering sense of internationalism, co-operation and social justice': see Elisabeth Stahle in *Biographical Dictionary of Modern Peace Leaders* (London: Greenwood Press, 1985), p. 105.

95 Bertha von Suttner (1843−1914), internationally renowned writer and lecturer, who devoted much of her life to working for peace. At the 1899 Hague conference, she was one of fifteen official journalists and the only woman. After the death of her friend Alfred Nobel in 1896 she helped to set up the Nobel Peace Prize, and was herself the recipient in 1905.

96 See pp. 57, 127−30 and 139.

97 Marion Wentworth Craig, 'War Brides; A Play in One Act', the *Century Magazine*, February 1915, pp. 527−44. Some quotations from the speeches given to the heroine illustrate the strength of this protest: 'Are we women never to get up out of the dust? You never asked us if we wanted this war, yet you ask us to ... drudge and slave, and wait, and agonise, lose our all, and go on bearing more men − and more − to be shot down! ... Well, if we are fit for that, we are fit to have a voice in the fate of the men we bear. If we can bring forth the men for the nation, we can sit with you in your councils and shape the destiny of the nation, and say whether it is to war or peace we give the sons we bear ... You think we are left at home because we are weak. Ah, no; we are strong ... Strong to keep the world going, to keep sacred the greatest things in life − love and home and work. To remind men of − peace.'

98 Emmeline Pethick-Lawrence (1867−1954). With her husband Frederick she worked for women's suffrage in the pre-war years; at first they were prominent in the WSPU, but in 1912 were expelled by the increasingly autocratic Christabel Pankhurst. From the outbreak of war she was a committed feminist pacifist; accepting an invitation to speak on women's suffrage in New York in October 1914, she became involved in the founding of the Women's Peace Party. She sailed to Europe for the Hague congress with Jane Addams and the other American delegates, and so was one of the few British women able to attend.

This speech was given at Kingsway Hall, London, on 8 June 1915, at a meeting organised by the United Suffragists, and was entitled 'The Women's Movement in Relation to the Present Crisis and the Immediate Future'.

99 Published by Allen & Unwin in 1916, with an introduction by Arnold Bennett. A 'new and enlarged edition' appeared in 1917.

100 P. Sargant Florence and J.R.L. Anderson, eds, *op. cit.*, p. 17.

Women and War

1 Talk prepared for 'Collegium Meeting', Central Hall, Westminster, 22 March 1915. Full text in Marshall Papers. In the event, Marshall was unable to attend because of illness, and her place was taken by Maude Royden. The Collegium series of meetings was dedicated to the religious aspects of the women's movement and peace. *Common Cause*, 26 March 1915.

2 'With eyes wide open, eyes which are willing to see'.

3 Literally, 'the pure fool, through compassion made wise'.

The Future of Women in Politics

1 Written some time in 1915 (undated Ms. in Marshall Papers), this article appeared in the *Labour Year Book* for 1916.

2 This is a reference to the EFF, see introduction p. 9, and reflects Marshall's determination that the alliance with Labour must survive the war.

Militarism versus Feminism

The original notes have been reproduced in appropriate order among those by the present editors, and except for those which consist solely or mainly of bibliographic references, are identified by an asterisk. The bibliographic references have been expanded where possible (using the *British Museum General Catalogue of Printed Books to 1955*) from the very abbreviated form of author's surname and short title, which was often all that was provided originally. We are impressed by the extent and breadth of the reading involved, and especially by the mention made of a number of books on the history or condition of women which are unknown to our generation. When time permits, we hope to follow up on some of these leads.

Other information, except where otherwise identified or of our own knowledge, has been obtained from *The Dictionary of National Biography*, *Who Was Who*, *Encyclopedia Britannica*, *Biographical Dictionary of Modern Peace Leaders*, Harold Josephson, ed (London: Greenwood Press, 1985).

1 A letter from Allen & Unwin, in response to an enquiry by the editors, indicates that they no longer have any records of correspondence which may have resulted from this invitation.

2 Sir Edward Grey: see Introduction, note 21.

3 Cloudesley Brereton, 'The Prussianisation of Germany', the *Common Cause*, 5 February 1915, p. 697 (Problems of War and Peace series).

4 General Friedrich Adam Julius von Bernhardi of Germany. The quotation is from the article, 'What I Found Out in the House of a German Prince', by an English governess, the *Fortnightly*, Vol. 103, January 1915, p. 78. General von Bernhardi is described there as conceited, formidable, ruthless and brutal-looking, 'the very type of militarism in flesh and blood', who considered the English 'beyond the pale', and despised women.

5 Fanny Smart, 'Open Letter; Women and Defence', the *Englishwoman*, January 1915, pp. 76—80. The author argues that in the conditions of modern war it is impossible for women and children to be protected as they were in the warfare of feudal times. In 1914, when a city is evacuated by the military, there is no organisation to protect those left behind. This makes nonsense of the theory that woman's place is in the home, and that man is her defender. She outlines a scheme to organise the women of a community so that in an emergency they would gather themselves together with the children and old people, with emergency rations and arms, to negotiate with the victorious forces and defend themselves if necessary. There is an interesting parallel between this analysis and that in an article by Judith Hicks Stiehm, 'The Protected, the Protector, the Defender', *Women's Studies International Forum*, Vol. 5, No. 3/4, 1982, pp. 367—76.

6   Mrs Hartley: see note 28.

7   John Stuart Mill (1806–73), English utilitarian philosopher and political economist whose partnership with feminist intellectual and writer Harriet Taylor (1807–58) resulted in the publication in 1869 of *The Subjection of Women*. The reference may also be to the first presentation in Parliament of a petition for women's suffrage in June 1869; the petition was organised by Barbara Bodichon and presented by Mill. Mill was elected to Parliament in 1865.

8   Probably a reference to the Women's Peace Party led by Jane Addams; copies of the promotional literature of this organisation are among Ogden's papers and were to be part of the longer work which he hoped to publish. The platform was quite similar to that put forward at the Women's International Congress at the Hague, 28 April–1 May 1915.

9   Sir James George Scott (1851–1935) was an administrator in Burma and spent most of his life there, writing prolifically about the country.

10   Carrie Chapman Catt (1859–1947), American feminist, President of the National American Women's Suffrage Association, 1901–04, and founder and first President of the International Women's Suffrage Alliance: a brilliant organiser and administrator. See e.g. Flexner, *op. cit.*

11   H. Fielding Hall, *The Soul of a People* (London: Richard Bentley & Son, 1898); and *A People at School* (London: Macmillan, 1906). Hall's books show him as an astute and almost sympathetic observer. The connection which emerges between peace, equality of status (not identity of roles) between the sexes, a non-hierarchical polity and a religion which is uncensorious but practises what it preaches is striking. Hall is clearly moved by what he sees — moved but not changed; he remains convinced that militarism is a higher stage of civilisation.

12   Elizabeth W. Andrew and Katherine C. Bushnell, *The Queen's Daughters in India*, with prefatory letters by Mrs Josephine E. Butler and Mr Henry J. Wilson, MP (London: Morgan & Scott, 1899). The authors were American social activists who visited India in 1892 and succeeded in publicising the legalisation and regulation of the prostitution of native women for the 'benefit' of the British soldier. This was seen by feminists as a continuation of the Contagious Diseases Acts which had been suspended in 1883 and abolished in England in 1886 as a result of the courageous

campaign by Josephine Butler. The notorious memorandum referred to here was in fact withdrawn as a result of the publicity, but only a few years later similar regulations were reintroduced. The reduction of venereal disease was of course the avowed rationale behind all such regulations; one cannot help but feel that implicit in them is also the Victorian horror of homosexuality and masturbation, evils from which the British male must be guarded by the sacrifice of women to satisfy his 'natural' appetites.

13 Sir William Wedderburn, 'An Indian Entente', *New Statesman*, 6 March 1915, pp. 531–2: the letter speaks of the need for a greater understanding between the peoples of Britain and of India, and suggests this could be best accomplished by 'women of progressive sympathies, both here and in India, who in the last few years have organised themselves into powerful societies, and undertaken extended work for the public good'. A national federation of such societies could, he feels, have an immeasurable influence for good on public opinion.

14 Leonard T. Hobhouse, *Morals in Evolution: a Study in Comparative Ethics*, 2 vols (London: Chapman & Hall, 1906), Vol. 1, p. 161.

*15 Sir George Laurence Gomme, in his *Folklore as an Historical Science*, The Antiquary's Books, J.C. Fox, ed (London: Methuen, 1904), marshals the latest evidence on this subject.

16 Sebald Rudolf Steinmetz was a German ethnologist writing at the end of the nineteenth and beginning of the twentieth centuries. We have not been able to identify the author Hales.

17 Edward A. Westermarck, *Origin and Development of Moral Ideas* (London: Macmillan, 1916). Chapter on 'The Subjection of Wives', Vol. 1, pp. 657–69.

18 Thornstein B. Veblen, *The Instinct of Workmanship and the State of the Industrial Arts* (New York: Macmillan, 1914).

*19 Even those who would not accept the theory of a 'peaceful stage' are driven to adopt the hypothesis of a peaceful 'lowland' population, perennially being 'eaten up' by warlike 'hillsmen', as, for instance, in the account of primitive warfare in Colonel F.N. Maude, *War and the World's Life* (London: Smith, Elder & Co., 1907), pp. 3–5.

20 Col. Philip R.T. Gurdon, *The Khasis*, with an introduction by Sir Charles Lyall (London: David Nutt, 1907), especially pp. 5 and 25.

21   Herbert Spencer (1820—1903), radical philosopher and Wesleyan dissenter; from 1848 sub-editor of *The Economist.*

22   Sir William Wilson Hunter, *Annals of Rural Bengal,* 3 vols, 7th ed (London: Smith & Elder, 1897; originally published 1868—72), Vol. 1, p. 217.

23   Brian H. Hodgson, *Miscellaneous Essays Relating to Indian Subjects,* Truebner's Oriental series (London: Truebner & Co., 1880), Vol. 1, p. 150.

24   Herbert Spencer, *Principles of Sociology,* 3 vols, Vol. 2, p. 633. (Vols 6—8 of his *A System of Synthetic Philosophy,* (London: Williams & Northgate, 1876—96).

25   Elie Reclus, *Primitive Folk: Studies in Comparative Ethnology* (London: Walter Scott, 1889), p. 108. 'Ross' is probably Sir James Clark Ross (1800—62), Arctic explorer who discovered the magnetic pole, and in 1848—49 commanded the *Enterprise* in the expedition for the relief of Sir John Franklin.

26   Berthold C. Seemann, *Narrative of the Voyage of the 'Herald' during the years 1845—51 . . . Being a Circumnavigation of the Globe, and Three Cruises to the Arctic Regions in Search of Sir J. Franklin,* 2 vols (London, 1853), Vol. 2, p. 66.

27   Murdoch, *Ann. Rep. Bur. Eth.,* IX, p. 413. We have not been able to identify this journal but reference to the abbreviations list in *World List of Scientific Periodicals published in the years 1900—60* (London: Butterworth, 1963), shows a likely full title to be *Annual Reports of the Bureau of Ethnology.*

28   Catherine Gasquoine Hartley, *The Truth About Women* (London: Eveleigh Nash, 1913), p. 170.

29   Westermarck, *op. cit.,* pp. 683—4.

30   Walter M. Gallichan, *Women Under Polygamy* (London: Holden & Hardingham, 1914), p. 16, and Hobhouse, *op. cit.,* Vol. 1, p. 252.

31   William Robertson Smith (1846—94), Scottish Semitic scholar, and student of comparative religion and social anthropology; in 1891 became joint editor of the *Encyclopedia Britannica.* The reference is probably to his *Kinship and Marriage in Early Arabia* (Cambridge: Cambridge University Press, 1885).

32   *Encyclopedia Britannica,* 11th ed, 1910—11, s.v. 'Arabia', by Rev. Griffithes Wheeler Thatcher.

33   S. Lane Poole, *The Speeches and Tabletalk of the Prophet Mohammad,* chosen and translated with introduction and notes, Golden Treasury Series (London: Macmillan, 1882), p. 161.

34 John M. Robertson, *The Evolution of States: An Introduction to English Politics* (London: Watts & Co., 1912), p. 151.

35 William H. Prescott, *History of the Reign of Ferdinand and Isabella the Catholic* (London, 1838), pp. 187–8.

36 Reinhart P.A. Dozy, *Historia de los Musulmanes Espanoles hasta la Conquista de Andalucia por los Almoravides*, 4 vols (Madrid, 1877), Vol. 3.

37 Henry Havelock Ellis, *Studies in the Psychology of Sex* (Philadelphia: F.A. Davis Co., 1910), Vol. 6: *Sex in Relation to Society*, p. 393. Havelock Ellis's writings on sex were enormously influential in his time, especially in intellectual and avant-garde circles, and did a great deal to make it a fit topic for scientific and sociological examination. He was a close friend of Olive Schreiner's.

*38 See also Mrs Archibald (Ethel) Colquhoun's remarks in, *The Vocation of Woman* (London: Macmillan, 1913), p. 172.

39 E. Amélineau, *La Morale Egyptienne Quinze Siècles avant notre ère; étude sur le papyrus de Boulaq*, No. 4 (Paris, 1892), p. 194.

40 George H. Perris, *A Short History of War and Peace*, Home University Library of Modern Knowledge (London: Williams & Northgate, 1911).

41 Gallichan, *op. cit.*, p. 36.

42 Revillout, *Journal Asiatique*, 1906, p. 57.

43 Sir James Donaldson, *Woman: Her Position and Influence in Ancient Greece and Rome, and Among the Early Christians* (London: Longmans, 1907).

44 *Ibid.*, p. 28.

45 Westermarck, *op. cit.*, Vol. 1, p. 669.

46 Maude, *op. cit.*, p. 243.

47 John A. Cramb, *Reflections on the Origin and Destiny of Imperial Britain* (London: Macmillan, 1900), p. 117.

48 William E.H. Lecky, *History of European Morals from Augustus to Charlemagne*, authorised copyright edition, 2 vols (London: Longmans, 1911; originally published 1869).

49 Jael (Judges, Chapter 4).

50 Johann J. Winckelmann wrote extensively on ancient art in the late eighteenth and nineteenth centuries.

51 Lecky, *op. cit.*, Vol. 2, p. 383.

52 Mother of the Gracchi: Cornelia, mother of Tiberius Sempronius Gracchus and Gaius Sempronius Gracchus, both of whom died violent deaths soon after becoming tribunes of Rome in 132 B.C. and 121 B.C. respectively.

53 John W. Graham, *Evolution and Empire* (London: Headley Bros., 1912). Graham was a Quaker, Principal of Dalton

Hall, Manchester, 1897–1924, and Professor at Swarthmore College, Pennsylvania, 1925–26. He wrote the official history of the No Conscription Fellowship, *Conscription and Conscience* (London: Allen & Unwin, 1922).

54   G. Ferrero, *Militarism* (London: Ward, Lock & Co., 1902), p. 93.

55   *Ibid.*, p. 134.

56   William James (1842–1910), lecturer in philosophy at Edinburgh University, Professor of philosophy at Harvard. His *The Moral Equivalent to War*, from *Memories and Studies* (London: Longmans, 1911), was reprinted as one of the Classics of Non-Violence series by the Peace Pledge Union, (London, 1943).

*57   'No society which preserves any tincture of Christian institutions is likely to restore to married women the personal liberty conferred on them by the middle Roman law', says Sir Henry Maine in *Ancient Law: Its Connection with the Early History of Society, and its Relation to Modern Ideas* (London, 1861), p. 158. Cf. Charles Kingsley's dictum: 'There will never be a good world for women until the last remnant of the Canon Law is civilised off the earth.'

58   The quotation is from *The Excursion*, Book 4.

59   Havelock Ellis, *op. cit.*, p. 397.

60   George Nathaniel, Marquess Curzon of Kedleston (1859–1925), Viceroy of India, 1898–1905; Lord Privy Seal, 1915; President of the Anti-Suffrage League.

      Wilhelm II's views on women were summed up by Charlotte Perkins Gilman as the Kaiser's four Ks – Küche, Kinder, Kirche, Kleider. (Cookery, children, church, clothes.) See *The Man-made World* (New York: Charlton Co., 1911), p. 87.

61   Albert L. Guerard, *French Civilisation in the XIXth Century: A Historical Introduction* (London: T. Fisher Unwin, 1914), p. 65.

62   John Holland Rose, *Life of Napoleon I*, 2 vols (London: George Bell & Sons, 1902), Vol. 1, p. 291.

63   Moisei Y. Ostrogorsky, *The Rights of Women: A Comparative Study in History and Legislation* (London: Swan Sonnenchein & Co., 1893), p. 209. Ostrogorsky (1854–1919) was a Russian political scientist, best known for a work on British and American politics, *Democracy and the Origin of Political Parties*, translated from the French by F. Clarke (London: Macmillan, 1902).

*64   'It was left to the genius of Napoleon to establish the system of 'maisons de tolérance' which had so great an influence over modern Europe during a large part of the last century' — Havelock Ellis, *op. cit.*, p. 249.

65 Paul Esmein, French legal scholar and part author of *Traité practique de droit civil français*, published 1925—34.

66 Ferrero, *op. cit.*, pp. 201—37.

67 Henry Duff Traill and James S. Mann, *Social England: A Record of the Progress of the People*, 6 vols (London: Cassell & Co., 1901—04), Vol. 2, p. 193. Sir John Arundel had desecrated a convent near Southampton, and among the women so callously drowned were the nuns whom he had captured. His ship was wrecked on the coast of Ireland. As good pacifists we refrain (with great difficulty) from making the obvious comment.

68 See note 7.

69 Lester F. Ward was a sociologist and paleobotanist, writing mainly between 1880 and 1910 in New York. It was to him that Charlotte Perkins Gilman dedicated her *The Man-made World* (see note 105).

70 See note 7.

71 Walter L. Blease, *The Emancipation of Englishwomen* (London: Constable, 1910), p. 138.

72 Walter Bagehot (1826—77), English economist and journalist, editor of the *Economist* from 1860—77. Best known for his *The English Constitution* (London: Chapman & Hall, 1867), and *Physics and Politics, or Thoughts on the Application of the Principles of 'Natural Selection' and 'Inheritance' to Political Society* (London: H.S. King & Co., 1872).

*73 *Physics and Politics*, p. 78. It is significant that Dr McDougall, one of the few modern psychologists who has written on the social psychology of war, refers to Bagehot's 'brilliant essay' (William McDougall, *An Introduction to Social Psychology*, London: Methuen, 1908, p. 283, on the Instinct of Pugnacity); while Professor J. Shield Nicholson writing during the war (*Economic Journal*, December 1914, p. 548) refers in unqualified terms to Bagehot's 'perennial freshness'. Bagehot, like Mill, is of importance as having influenced two generations of University thought. *Physics and Politics* is still a *sine qua non* for any youth who aspires to an Oxford scholarship!

74 The sufferings of the civilian populations in Belgium and Poland in 1914—15 are well known. That winter there was severe fighting in the province of Galicia between the Russians and the Germans. Scarborough was one of the

English cities shelled by the Germans on 16 December 1914. A notorious case in Cardiff had seen the imprisonment of five women under an extension of the Defence of the Realm Act of 28 August 1914 which had put areas of the country with large military camps under martial law. In an attempt to control prostitution, an order had been promulgated at Cardiff 'restricting certain women to their own homes within certain hours', and the five women who were caught disobeying were arrested and tried under martial law. The Defence of the Realm Act was subsequently amended to give all civilians the right of trial by jury. See *Women's Dreadnought* (journal of the East London Federation of Suffragettes, edited by Sylvia Pankhurst), 5 December 1914, p. 150; 12 December, p. 155); 9 January 1915, p. 175; and the *Common Cause*, 15 January 1915, p. 650; 26 February 1915, p. 729.

75 Jane Ellen Harrison, *'Homo Sum': Being a Letter to an Anti-Suffragist from an Anthropologist*, 2nd ed (London: NUWSS, 1913).

76 Gomme, *op. cit.*, p. 257.

77 Ethel Snowden, *The Feminist Movement* (London: Collins, 1913), p. 38.

*78 'Und ueberhaupt das Parlamentieren, worin the [sic] Frau Meisterin ist' (Franz Mueller-Lyer, *Phasen der Liebe; eine Soziologie des Verhaltnisses der Geschlechter*, München 1913, p. 190). [The sense of the quotation is: '. . . and to sum up, haggling, in which the woman is a champion . . .' Ed.]

*79 Sir John Robert Seeley, *The Expansion of England: Two Courses of Lectures* (London: Macmillan, 1883), p. 128. The same thing has been pointed out by Dean Inge recently with even more force.

[William Ralph Inge, Dean of St Paul's (1860–1954); we have not been able to identify the source of this reference – Ed.]

80 Admiral Alfred T. Mahan (1840–1914), American naval officer and historian who wrote extensively on the importance of sea power.

81 The Women's Co-operative Guild was founded in 1883 as an auxiliary of the British Consumer Co-operative movement; it embodied the ideas of social feminism – a belief in the nurturant and co-operative role of women in all spheres of life, including international affairs. Margaret Llewellyn Davies was General Secretary of the Guild and its leading inspiration from 1889–1922. (See Naomi Black, 'The

Mother's International: The Women's Co-operative Guild and Feminist Pacifism', *Women's Studies International Forum*, Vol. 7, No. 6, pp. 467–76.)

82 Charles Kingsley (1819–75) believed that war had a regenerating influence on society, and was the author of a tract, *Brave Words to Brave Soldiers*, distributed to the army during the Crimean War.

*83 Rose, *Life of Napoleon*, Vol. 1, p. 291. Five pages earlier Dr Rose informs the youth of England that Napoleon 'united in his own person the ablest qualities of the statesman and the warrior!' De Tocqueville puts it more clearly — 'He was as great as a man could be without virtue.'

84 Seeley, *op. cit.*, p. 3.

85 The only possible source for this reference which we can find is: Charlotte Wilson and Helen M. Blagg, *Women and Prisons*, Fabian Tract No. 163, London, 1912.

86 Edmond Gore Holmes, *What Is and What Might Be: A Study of Education in General and Elementary Education in Particular* (London: Constable, 1911), p. 50.

87 R. Seidel, in the *Cambridge Magazine*, 15 November 1913.

88 Thomas Arnold (1795–1842), English educationalist and historian; headmaster of Rugby School, Warwickshire (founded 1567), from 1828–42, where he liberalised the curriculum and carried out many reforms.

89 *Quarterly Review*, Vol. 102, No. 204, October 1957, pp. 330–54. The article is a review of two books about Rugby School, and compares the 'bold and manly games' to the 'gymnastics of the sages of antiquity'. Football is said to 'mimic war' and to encourage 'that dogged determination to win, that endurance of pain, that bravery of combative spirit by which the adult is trained to face the cannon ball with equal alacrity'.

90 Lionel Portman, *Hugh Rendal: A Public School Story* (London: Alston Rivers, 1905).

91 Dulwich College, another English public school, in South London, founded in 1605.

92 Maria Montessori, *The Montessori Method* (London: William Heinemann, 1912), p. 363.

93 Chartist riots, 1838: Chartism arose out of the appalling conditions and the exploitation of workers which characterised the Industrial Revolution in Britain, and got its name from the 'People's Charter' which embodied its surprisingly modern-sounding demands.

*94 Maude, *op. cit.* The italics are ours.

95   The Volunteer movement in Britain arose in the 1850s in response to the panic over the supposed ill intentions of Napoleon III of France, when civilian volunteers received military training in their leisure hours. After the Franco-Prussian war in 1870, the British Army was reformed and reorganised and an Army reserve created. (G.M. Trevelyan, *English Social History*, London: Longmans, 1942, p. 550.)

96   So we live, so we live, so we all live here;
            Mornings with the brandy, noon-time with the beer;
            Evenings with the girls in the night quarters.
       The author's German is not too accurate: the last line should read: 'Des Abends bei *dem* Maedle in *dem* Nacht Quartier'.

97   Most probably a quotation from *The War and Democracy*, by John Dover Wilson, R.W. Seton-Watson, Alfred E. Zimmern and Arthur Greenwood (London: Macmillan, 1914).

98   Ethel (Mrs Archibald) Colquhoun, *The Vocation of Woman* (London: Macmillan, 1913).

99   Sinclair Kennedy, *The Pan-Angles: A Consideration of the Federation of the Seven English-speaking Nations* (London: Longmans, 1914).

100   Olive Schreiner, *Woman and Labour* (London: T. Fisher Unwin, 1911), p. 56. (Reprinted with a preface by Jane Graves, London: Virago Press, 1978.)

101   Bernhardi (see note 4), *Germany and the Next War*, translated by Allen Powles (London: Edward Arnold, 1912), p. 131.

102   Cicely M. Hamilton, *Marriage as a Trade* (London: Chapman & Hall, 1909), p. 67. (Reprinted with an introduction by Jane Lewis, London: The Women's Press, 1981.)

103   *op. cit.*, p. 11.

104   Ellen Key, *The Woman Movement*, translated from the Swedish by Mamah Bouton Borthwick, with an introduction by Havelock Ellis (London and New York: Putnam, 1912).

105   Charlotte Perkins Gilman in *The Man-made World, or Our Androcentric Culture* (New York: Charlton Co., 1911; reprinted New York and London: Johnson Reprint Co., 1971). Quoted in Anne Wiltsher, *Most Dangerous Women* (London: Pandora Press, 1985), p. 45. The quotation, to be found on p. 211 of the 1971 reprint edition; later, on p. 215, we read, '. . . warfare, at its best, retards human progress; at its worst, obliterates it'.

106   Romain Rolland (1866–1944), French novelist, dramatist and essayist, who was deeply involved in the social, political

and spiritual affairs of his time. The works referred to are: *Jean Christophe*, 10 vols (Paris, 1905–12), and *Au dessus de la Melée* (Paris, 1915), which won the Nobel Prize for Literature in that year and was translated by C.K. Ogden as *Above the Battle* (London: Allen & Unwin, 1915).

107 Gerhart Hauptmann (1862–1946), German dramatist, awarded the Nobel Prize for Literature in 1912, whose work is marked by a deep concern for suffering. The first chapter of Rolland's *Above the Battle* is 'An Open Letter to Gerhart Hauptmann'. Ogden is here reflecting on the irony that places two great humanitarians on opposing sides in the war.

108 'And on account of life, one loses the reason for living.' Rolland expands the sense of this quotation as follows: 'What is the value of life when you have saved it at the price of all that is worth living for?' (Ogden's translation of *Above the Battle*, p. 53.)

Extracts from Militarism, Feminism and the Birthrate

1 William Graham Sumner, *War and other essays*, Oxford University Press, London, 1911, p. 348.

2 This is the article referred to in the introduction, note 52, which was signed by 'M. Sargant Florence' and 'C.K. Ogden'.

3 'The degrading episode' at Plymouth seems to refer to a suggestion that the notorious Contagious Diseases Act should be re-enacted in an attempt to control venereal disease among military personnel stationed in the area, reported with indignation in the *Women's Dreadnought*, 17 October 1914 and the *Common Cause*, 16 October 1914. For Plymouth see note 74 to *Militarism versus Feminism*.

4 A 'diplodocus', according to the *Encyclopedia Britannica*, is an extinct dinosaur, the longest land animal that ever lived but with a very small brain.

5 See the discussion on education in Chapter IV of *Militarism versus Feminism*.

6 John William Graham (1854–1932): see note 53 to *Militarism versus Feminism*. The quotation which follows is not identified.

7 *Towards Permanent Peace: A Record of the Women's International Conference at the Hague, April 28–May 1, 1915*, p. 20,

in an article by the editor of the *Cambridge Magazine*.

8 Maude Royden (1876—1956), member of NUWSS Executive and gifted speaker for the cause of women's suffrage; a convinced pacifist, she resigned from the Executive and the editorship of the *Common Cause* at the time of the split in 1915. She was most interested in the religious and ethical aspects of pacifism, and in 1917 became assistant preacher at the City Temple, London (her own Church of England refusing to accept women preachers). She later travelled widely as an interdenominational preacher.

Books by Vera Brittain

Testament of Youth

One of the most famous and best loved autobiographies of the First World War, *Testament of Youth* is both a passionate record of those agonizing years and a loving memorial to a lost generation. In spirit and impact it is as powerful as those other classics of the First World War, *All Quiet on the Western Front* and *Goodbye to All That*.

Testament of Experience

Vera Brittain continues the story of those who survived the devastation of the First World War, once again interlacing private experience with the wide sweep of public events. Personal happiness in marriage and the birth of children, pride in her work as writer and campaigner are set against the fears, frustrations and achievements of the years 1925–50, one of the most crucial and stirring periods the world has known.

Testament of Friendship

Vera Brittain tells the story of the woman who helped her to survive the tragic loss of those she most loved— the writer Winifred Holtby. They met at Oxford immediately after the war and their friendship continued through Vera's marriage and their separate but parallel writing careers, until Winifred's untimely death at the age of thirty-seven. *Testament of Friendship* records a perfect friendship between two women of courage and determination.

The Face of War

Martha Gellhorn

Martha Gellhorn's career as a war correspondent began in Spain in 1937. From then on her first-hand experiences of the tragedy and suffering of war—in Finland, China, Europe, South East Asia and Central America— were to become the subject of countless articles unique for their immediacy and range, each conveying 'the exact sound, smell, gestures' of the people and events she observed.

First published in 1959, updated in the late 1960s and now again in 1985, *The Face of War* is a remarkable anthology of Martha Gellhorn's writings from the front-line of war. This new edition brings her work up to date, including articles on the Six-Day Arab-Israeli War of 1967, on El Salvador and Nicaragua, and portrays brilliantly the human cost of war wherever it occurs: 'Memory and imagination, not nuclear weapons, are the great deterrents.' A work of vision and compassion, *The Face of War* is an outstanding portrait of war in our tim and a passionate condemnation of its folly.

'More than any journalist I **horn has elevated war report** **to humanity, life and peace. H** *of War* **is a classic'—*John Pilger**

Over Our Dead Bodies: Women Against the Bomb

Edited by Dorothy Thompson

We are beginning to think the unthinkable—that there could be a nuclear war in our lifetime. Yet politicians and the media tell us that we lack the expertise to argue against nuclear weapons. This book has an abundance of facts—on nuclear weapons, deterrence theory, civil defence, the nuclear arms race, alternative defence strategy. But it insists too that questions of peace and war are questions of morality and politics, that we are all capable of judging the issues and seeing the dangers— the militarisation of our society, the dehumanising of the 'enemy', the paralysis of the imagination induced by contemplating a nuclear future.

These are the voices of deeply concerned women: historians, novelists, politicians, philosophers, women in the peace movement and the peace cam~   n working in arms factories. They don'~   e
        ~~ who passionately wan*
             ~la fo~~
            know, Martha Gell-
         ng to a commitment
      ler brilliant *The Face*
                                           ~~ust

Contributors: Alison Assiter, Jeanette Buirski, Angela Carter, Gay Clifford, Janet Dubé, Lisa Foley, Jill Liddington, Maggie Lowry, Connie Mansueto, Bel Mooney, Marjorie Mowlam, Ann Pettitt, Cathy Porter, Beryl Ruehl, Myrtle Solomon, Kate Soper, Marian Sugden, Dorothy Thompson, Hilary Wainwright, Maxine Wombwell, Suzanne Wood.